Be Happy, Be Free, Dance!

A Holocaust Survivor's Message to His Grandchildren

Intentional Productions
Pasadena, California   2005

Be Happy, Be Free, Dance!

A Holocaust Survivor's Message to His Grandchildren

Richard Weilheimer
Edited by Claire Gorfinkel

Book and cover design by Anne Richardson-Daniel

Library of Congress Cataloging-in-Publication Data

Weilheimer, Richard, 1931-
  Be happy, be free, dance! : Holocaust survivor's message to his grandchildren / Richard Weilheimer ; edited by Claire Gorfinkel.
     p. cm.
  Summary: "A child survivor of the Holocaust, Richard Weilheimer describes life in pre-WW II Germany, the rise of Nazism, and his family's deportation to the misery of Camp de Gurs in Vichy-controlled France. Rescued by the Quakers, Richard established himself in the United States. Forty years later he challenges his grandchildren to live fully and resist intolerance"--Provided by publisher.
  ISBN-13: 978-0-9648042-7-2 (alk. paper)
  1. Weilheimer, Richard, 1931- 2. Holocaust, Jewish (1939-1945)--Germany--Personal narratives. 3. Jewish children in the Holocaust--Germany--Personal narratives. 4. Jewish children in the Holocaust--France--Personal narratives. I. Gorfinkel, Claire. II. Title. DS135.G5W396 2005
  940.53'18'0943--dc22
                              2005018282

ISBN 978-09648042-7-2

© Richard Weilheimer, 2005

No part of this book may be reproduced or transmitted in any form or by any means, electronic or mechanical without written permission from the author, except for brief quotations or reviews.

Intentional Productions
PO Box 94814, Pasadena, CA 91109
... publishing stories of courage ...
human responses to adversity and evil.

With gratitude to Sheila, whose love, patience and help made this book possible and to the rest of my loving family who urged me to commit my memory to paper.

Men, Women, Children, Masses for the gas chambers
Advancing toward horror beneath the whip of the executioner
Your sad Holocaust is engraved in history
And nothing shall purge your deaths from our memories
For our memories are your only grave

From a bronze plaque in the former Jewish Ghetto of Venice

Dedicated to Holocaust Remembrance
and the memory of my dear *Mutti* and *Papi*,

Lilly Wetzler Weilheimer   1902 – Gurs, 1941

Maximilian Weilheimer   1887 – Sobibor, 1943

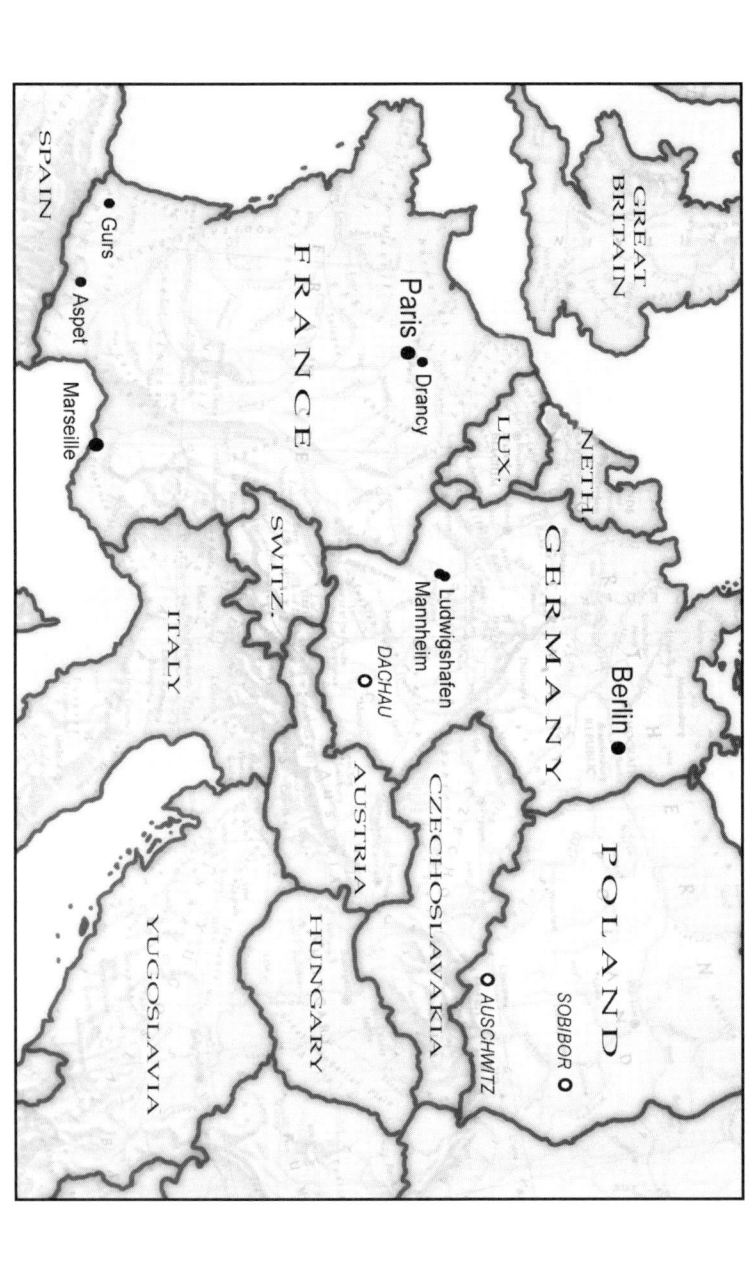

Table of Contents

Foreword i

1. Background - The Rise of Nazism 1
2. My Family and Early Childhood 5
3. *Kristallnacht* and the Start of World War II 15
4. Deportation to *Camp de Gurs* 29
5. *La Maison des Pupilles* 49
6. Path to Freedom 79
7. A New Life 99
8. After High School and Into Another War 119
9. Settling Down 131
10. In Touch with the Past 141
11. My Mission, My Command 155
12. Appendix 165

Foreword

For many years I refused to talk about the Holocaust. I broke my self-imposed silence in order to describe that nightmare of history known as the *Shoah* as I experienced it, so that my family will know their connection to murdered relatives. As a Survivor, a primary source of history, I must bear witness, to speak for those who no longer can, about the Nazi's attempt to exterminate the entire Jewish "race," religion and culture. Equally, I feel compelled to recognize and speak about those few brave individuals, who risked safety, freedom, their own and their families' lives in a desire to do the right thing – the humanitarian, moral thing – by helping Jews: feeding them, providing shelter and aiding them in their attempts to escape from the jaws of death.

My children's heritage does not begin with me. Their genes are linked to generations of grandparents and relatives they never knew. My sons and their children deserve to know that despite Hitler's rhetorical diatribes and obsessive efforts to eradicate Jewish life, they are the scions of esteemed families, deeply rooted in German-Jewish culture and traditions. I do not expect them to comprehend the tragedy – I cannot. No one can. The magnitude and horror defies explanation. But memory must be respected. As we look to the future, we must not forget the past. Much has been written about the *Shoah* but history books are products of scholars, while memoirs are the personal recollections of individuals, evidence of our particular ordeals and our unique ways of coping. I must record what is etched in my mind so that it will not be forgotten. It should remind and enlighten my children and succeeding generations about the evils and cruelty I witnessed and the lessons we must learn.

Until I was able, willing and *driven* to speak about the Holocaust forty-five years after immigrating to the United States, I had not read a book, seen a movie or viewed a television production or documentary dealing with this subject. I distanced myself from any conversation when the Holocaust was even mentioned, thus unwittingly preserving my unfiltered memories. My psychological state acted as an invisible fence, keeping what I had experienced in my subconscious, in the innermost corners of my brain, protecting it from contamination.

My silence was also a way of hiding. It was an unobtrusive safety net which allowed me to keep my past locked in a private compartment, to be recalled but not revealed. My close friends knew of my origin and my "refugee" status but they never requested details, which I was not yet able to share.

In 1988, as a result of hearing a Survivor speak on the fiftieth anniversary of *Kristallnacht*, I could no longer keep my experience to myself. I was finally ready to share my particular story, and my recollections were clear, unfiltered by outside influences. While some scars will always remain, this new-found openness had therapeutic side effects. In the process of recalling my story, at first certain aspects or sequences seemed to be missing or forgotten. However, when I started talking about point "A" and proceeded to point "C," somehow "B" came to mind and made the connection. This process of stirring and reviving a dormant memory felt strange and even uncomfortable at times. As I began speaking to students more frequently, to my amazement I experienced flashbacks from my subconscious psyche, recreating events which I witnessed. I began to question my memory and needed to reaffirm

Foreword

the validity of my stories. Through a series of coincidences, more than 50 years after the Holocaust I located several Survivors who were with me at various stages and we exchanged copies of oral testimonies that each of us had given separately to Steven Spielberg's *Survivors of the Shoah Visual History Foundation* interviewers and other archives. We also talked to each other about our common experiences. I was stunned and relieved to find that – even as our individual experiences differed – in almost every instance where fate had connected us, our independent recollections were alike, thus validating my regenerated memory.

Though my story is intact, it is important to recognize that the early events I am about to relate were seen through the eyes of a child, so details or understanding of complex situations may be missing. There is a particular incongruity between the stark misery of the adults' world and their efforts to maintain a near normal life for their children. For example, letters from our parents whom we left behind in a dismal Vichy concentration camp were filled with everyday micro-concerns, and cheerful descriptions.

It took many years before I was ready to commit my story to paper, but this text was inscribed on my mind a long time ago. It needed the urging of a loving family to release it and much effort on my part to relate and explain that which is inexplicable.

Germany was one of the world's most advanced nations. It is still incomprehensible how a learned society of doctors, scientists, educators, engineers, architects, industrialists and artists could have been harnessed to forge the most vicious, sadistic and efficient government-sponsored death industry mankind has ever conceived. Evil saw no boundaries. Composers wrote songs such as *"When Jewish Blood Squirts from the Knife, Things Go Twice As Well."* Artists illustrated children's textbooks depicting

Jews as vermin to be exterminated. Engineers built gas chambers and doctors performed cruel and heinous experiments on children and adults, causing slow, torturous deaths. Educated German citizens gleefully recorded body counts of Jews as their lifeless corpses piled up in ditches amidst the mantra of automatic weapons. All contributed to this failed humanity which had become anchored to a fanatic anti-Semitic ideology relegating Jews to the status of *"untermenschen"* – subhuman creatures whose very existence was said to threaten Germany.

A partial explanation arises from Germany's defeat in the First World War and the harsh consequences of the Versailles Treaty, which in turn led to unemployment and other hardships among the population. This helped form the fertile womb from which hatred was nurtured. The National Socialist Party responded by seeking a scapegoat to arouse the masses. Having been hated and persecuted for more than two thousand years, Jews were the pre-packaged, ever-ready, standby villains. We were held responsible for every failure and misfortune that befell Germany and its people, from losing the war to the collapse of the economy, not because of anything we had done, but simply because we were Jews.

Nazi racial policies declared that Jews were an inferior alien people compared to the homogeneous, superior Aryan "master race." Even converts to Christianity and non-practicing Jews were deemed "racially defective" through standards set by the pseudo-science of "eugenics." And while not everyone was a Nazi, most Germans did nothing to intervene, choosing to ignore the evil and injustice around them so long as their own social group was not victimized. Others saw the Nazi phenomenon as a crazed ambition which would soon self-destruct or implode before it could take root. State-sponsored anti-Semitism had long been prevalent in various countries, but this was the first time that a total effort was made to eliminate all Jews. Previous policies had sometimes been: "You cannot live here as Jews"

Foreword

(conversion); or "You cannot live here" (expulsion). Hitler's final solution to the Jewish problem was: "You cannot live" (extermination).

History is the transmission of collective memories of humankind as perceived by individual witnesses and investigative scholars. As various bits of information come together, they form and preserve the events of life's journey. Indeed, history is a rear-view mirror reflecting the road we have traveled and the experiences we have had. Above all it identifies who we are and the moments that compelled us to act. But this "history" should really be called *"TheirStories."* Each of the six million Jews and five million others murdered by the Nazis had their own characteristic life and experiences. They were slaughtered one by one. Each death was individual. Those who survived have unique stories as well, although many were in similar situations. So it is urgent that survivors with stories still untold share their tales with generations yet unborn. We must dedicate ourselves to preserving these memories, and be vigilant as we entrust our legacy to the conscience of mankind, so that time and those who document it do not taint, distort or recast it.

When we speak of the fate of Jews during the Holocaust, the sickly, dirty, skeletal images of the dehumanized camp inmates comes to mind. It is important to attach human faces to the victims of atrocities and to remember that these were once happy, healthy, active and contributing members of society. Prior to the Holocaust, before they were stripped of civil, legal and basic human rights, including the right to live, they were people: husbands, wives, mothers, fathers, sons, daughters, friends and neighbors. They had families; they loved and frolicked among us.

Most of those who survived were able to build new lives, even though scars, fears, hurts and suspicions would always remain. Our memories of former lives, families and homes became haunting blocks in the process of forging a new existence. We were once children, but we were robbed of our childhood. We witnessed destruction and unimaginable cruelty. We lacked security and basic needs. We drifted in a sea of impotent, dehumanized people in a fanatically hostile environment. As a result, we tried to repress memories while assuming normality. We tried to explain some actions and phobias and our need for moments of isolation. We lived with wounds no one else saw but all Survivors understood, and worked to create a delicate balance between what we hoped to forget and what we needed to remember.

Although we did not always recognize it at the time, some "angels" also helped us, took us from one place and delivered us safely somewhere else. Some whom we never got to know entered our lives, disappeared and returned without notice, forming the links for our survival. Indeed, many of us would not be here to tell our stories if it were not for those righteous people of moral character and great courage in all countries and of all religions. Sadly, there were not enough, but given the penalty of death, it is surprising that anyone at all would have risked their neck for strangers. I don't know if I could have. Certainly I would have wanted to, but it was a dangerous choice when insanity ruled.

One ingredient of survival was faith: faith in ourselves and in the "angels" who crossed our paths even momentarily, and faith in a higher authority, even though the question of God's whereabouts and non-interference remain an unanswered and troubling dilemma. Of course, faith was not enough. Survival happened; it was mostly luck.

Having addressed thousands of school children and adults in classrooms and forums, I became more aware of their naiveté when they tried to understand the difficult predicament of German Jews. They often asked questions for which no simple answer could be given: "Why didn't the Jews just get out of Germany?" I saw that my audiences needed to hear my story in the context of what

Foreword

was going on in Germany and the world. I have therefore included some background information so that events which affected me can be better understood. But this is by no means a textbook; rather it is my personal experiences and impressions as I navigated through a murderous regime.

To have ended this account of my life at the point of immigration to the United States would not have told my complete story. Students have asked about my post-Nazi, post World War II life. They wanted to know how a ten and a half-year-old orphan functioned in America. How did I put my life together? How did I deal with my background? What effect did my past have? What motivated and helped me in my determination to move beyond that which would always stay in my mind? They were anxious to know if I had ever returned to Germany and my current feelings and attitude towards Germans. Questions kept coming and the need and obligation to explain and talk about this distant time urged me on.

The mission of the next generation is to remember and retell our stories. But if we are truly to deny Hitler his final victory, they must also "Be happy, Be free, Dance!"

1. Background - The Rise of Nazism

Anti-Semitism was present for generations in Germany, as it was throughout Europe, but it took on a more subtle form. Records of the Jewish presence in the region date back 1600 years, long before Germany became a unified nation. By the Nineteenth Century, Jews had become well integrated in mainstream society, prominent in business, professions, medicine, law, the arts, science, the armed forces, universities, politics and government. By 1933, eleven of Germany's thirty-seven Nobel Prize winners were Jews, even though they constituted less than 1% of the population.

In hindsight there is perfect vision, but when Hitler took over in 1933 it was not yet clear that the German legislative process could so easily be hijacked, or that people could be so thoroughly intimidated as to allow injustice to rule over law and order. The systematic humiliation and deprivation of Jews did not arise overnight but started slowly, and it was never seriously challenged from within or by the world's political and religious leaders. The tragic events that befell the Jews were perceived as the exclusive business of a sovereign entity. The sin of silence was global.

The Nazi Party began as a right-wing group known as the German Workers' Party, whose membership roster was dominated by strong-armed thugs and agitators with their own agenda. Their original purpose was to promote the rights of laborers and the underprivileged. Adolf Hitler became the leader and in 1923 he attempted to overthrow the fledgling Weimar Democratic Republic. Although his *Putsch* ended in failure and a five year prison sentence, the ten months he actually served was enough time to write *Mein Kampf* (My Struggle), his ideological roadmap for an authoritarian dictatorship.

There was never any mystery about Hitler's intentions, including his goal of rendering greater Germany entirely free of Jews. His publisher's promotional ads proclaimed "get to know Hitler through his book." While the Nazis exploited Germany's severe economic disaster and the decline in national pride, Hitler showed great talent in rousing emotions and promising redemption. Although the Nazis did not receive a clear majority in the election of 1932, they did get more votes than any other party, and Hitler was legally appointed Chancellor of Germany on January 30, 1933. The country became democratically and morally bankrupt.

The Nazis immediately dismembered the Democratic Republic and established a single legal political party. Within two months, the first concentration camp (primarily for political opponents) was operational at Dachau. Less than two weeks later, Germans were ordered to boycott Jewish businesses and professions, then Jewish hospital workers, civil service employees, school teachers and administrators were dismissed. In early May, orchestrated book-burnings took place, destroying texts written by Jews, about Jews and Jewish subjects. Hundreds of new laws deprived Jews of the ability to support their families and stripped them of their civil rights. They were forced to relinquish possessions and assets. And so it went: Jewish life, culture and economic strength diminished day by day. Meanwhile, the German population's passive consent enabled the government of the Third Reich to expand its evil agenda.

"The final solution to the Jewish problem," i.e. extermination, had not yet been devised so no one could possibly imagine the ultimate fate awaiting the Jews. The community was nevertheless devastated. Some families, seeing "the writing on the wall," left the country, while others who wanted to leave could not surmount the obstacles. Still others assumed that the Nazi barbarians would be dismissed in short order thus ending the tyranny. Their attachment to the culture and allegiance to Germany was often stronger than their Jewishness, and they believed that their prior contributions to the fatherland would be recognized and honored. Naiveté and wishful thinking clouded their judgment, even as the humiliations continued, and the hours and conditions under which they could shop, attend cultural events or cinemas, visit parks, or use public transportation were increasingly restricted. They were brutalized psychologically. Gentile neighbors acquiesced to despotism and abandoned common civility.

When German President Hindenburg died in 1934, Hitler proclaimed himself *Führer*, Leader. His fanatic charisma and venomous anti-Semitism captured and roused the German *Volk*. His vicious lies and accusations were repeated so often that they seemed to emit an aura of truth. The "Nuremberg Laws" of 1935 stripped Jews of their citizenship and all legal protections. Marriages and intimate relationships between Jews and Aryans were banned. In 1938 Jews were required to declare all their business holdings, which were subsequently confiscated and *Aryanized*. Jewish students were thrown out of public schools. The licenses of those lawyers and other professionals who were still practicing in the Jewish community were revoked. Identification cards and passports were replaced with ones in which every Jewish woman was assigned the middle name of "Sarah" and every Jewish man was required to take the middle name of "Israel." A huge red "J" for *Jude,* (Jew) was stamped on passports and I.D. cards. (Ironically, the red "J" had been suggested by the Swiss for the convenience of border guards and custom officials. Switzerland, evidently, had

Be Happy, Be Free, Dance!

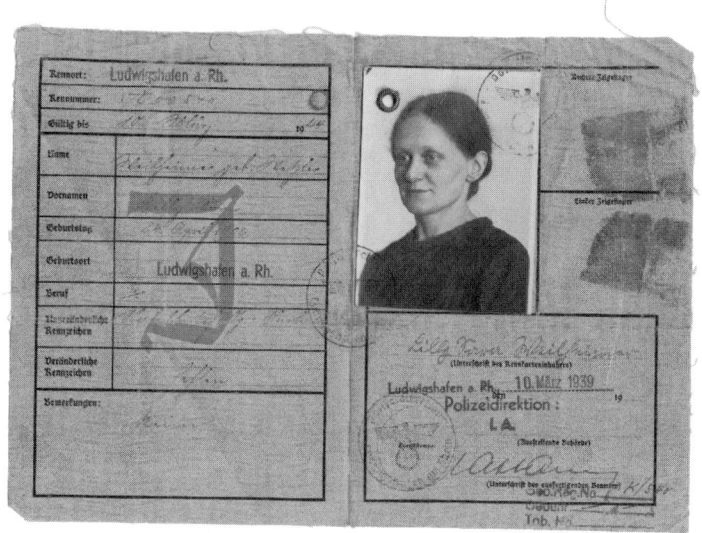

Mutti's ID card, with the middle name "Sara" and the "J" for Jude (Jew)

its fill of Jews trying to find a safe haven.) *Kristallnacht*, the first state-organized physical assaults on businesses, synagogues and homes took place on November 9, 1938.

Our opportunities and choices waned rapidly as the rape of our assets and our economic well-being made us undesirable as immigrants. Jews could no longer support themselves in a depression-era world. As life became more unbearable, indeed impossible, there was a flurry of activity: long lines at foreign consulates, frustrations, obstacles, delays, disappointments and then, finally, we were trapped. Emigration became impossible; there was no place to go.

What needs to be understood is that all this occurred in the open, in the midst of an advanced civilization. It was done with enthusiasm amid great publicity and propaganda by a shameless society. It was conceived with the knowledge of all Germans and carried out before the eyes of rest of the world.

2. *My Family and Early Childhood*

Now, as an aging adult, finally willing to face what I had for so long avoided, I find the window closed and there is nothing but darkness. How could I have failed to allow the rays of knowledge from penetrating, my yearnings to know from shedding light on that for which I have so little memory? All those years in which I suppressed thoughts of that terrible era are now gone, and they took with them all my relatives, their contemporaries and fellow immigrants who held intimate information of my immediate family, our community and the events that affected our lives. There are so many unanswered questions - so much I need to know - but there is no one to turn to. No one remains who is familiar with the early part of my life. No one recalls what I was too young to remember. I missed out on the awareness of my own childhood, of knowing the joys of my family before the war. I have only isolated, unconnected fragments of memory from those early days and so each recollection, no matter how inconsequential, is a valued link to that which I have lost. Each recalled event is now a treasure, not because of the occurrence but because it connects me with my lost family.

The Weilheimer family's origin can be traced to a small town near Nuremberg called Weilheim. In the early seventeenth century, one branch of the Weilheimers moved to what became known as the Palatinate in the west central part of the country. The men made their living at the limited options open to Jews: trading horses and peddling household items and fabrics. They walked from village to village hawking their wares from early Monday morning until Friday afternoon. Around 1820, when Jews were permitted to live in cities, most of the family settled in an industrial area on the Rhein River which became Ludwigshafen in 1852. There they started a building materials business, dealing in iron and other metals. My paternal great-grandfather, Solomon Weilheimer, was born in Dossenheim, Baden (near Heidelberg) but he moved to Ludwigshafen where he first became a shoemaker and then a merchant. My paternal grandfather, Seligman (Samuel) who died before my birth, was married to Fanny, nee Hartmann. He was the first Jewish City Counselor in Ludwigshafen from 1898 to 1910. Together they had seven children, one girl and six boys. Ernst died in 1908. Johanna (Jenny) died shortly before my birth in 1931. Richard was killed in action at the Somme during the First World War on September 3, 1916. Alfred (Fred) emigrated to the United States along with his wife Irma and their daughter Lotte, shortly after *Kristallnacht* on December 31, 1938. Besides my brother Ernst and me, they were the only Weilheimers who were not murdered in the concentration camps. My father Maximilian (Max), his brother Ludwig and his wife, my Aunt Tilde, were killed at Sobibor in 1943. My Uncle Sigmund (Muni) was murdered at Auschwitz in 1942. My father's first cousins, Flora, Wally and Paula were also murdered at Auschwitz and Karl died in Gurs.

I know little about my father's family, and it is a source of great sadness to me that I remember even less about my mother's. She was the eldest of five Wetzler children, raised in Ludwigshafen, where her father was a highly regarded leader and Cantor in the Jewish community. She was trained as a teacher, and before marrying my father, she ran a very successful private kindergarten. Her sister Nelly married Kurt Stern, and her sister Alice married Maurice Strassburger. Along with their sister Emmy, who

My Family and Early Childhood

Mutti (age 32), me, Mutti's mother (Oma) and her grandmother on her 85th birthday in 1934

was married to Frederick Rosenfelder (later Rosen, then Ralston) they all had the good fortune to emigrate to America in the late 1930s. Edgar, the youngest of the five Wetzler children and the only boy, also became a teacher – but the Nazis would not permit him to teach in a German school so he taught in the local Jewish school. Edgar was imprisoned in Dachau after *Kristallnacht* and upon his release in early 1939 he made his way to England where he was detained as an "Enemy Alien." He gained his release by volunteering to go to Australia to serve in their "Home Defense Force." He remained in Australia after the war, married and had a daughter. He died of a heart ailment at an early age.

Prior to the rise of Nazism my parents would have been considered "upper middle-class." My father was the secretary of the Jewish Community. I was born in Ludwigshafen November 21, 1931; my brother Ernst was born in Mannheim, December 11, 1935.

Mutti and Papi shortly after their wedding in 1930

From my limited early memories, I recall helping *Mutti* (mother) in the kitchen, doing little chores such as cranking the handle of a noodle machine into which she inserted her homemade dough to create the thin strands which would be part of our dinner. I recall sitting at the kitchen table helping her remove the dark inedible matter from a sack of lentils before they went into our soup. I always looked forward to meals that included boiled chestnuts mixed with a vegetable, most often brussel sprouts. *Mutti's* skills as a kindergarten teacher were evident in the creative arts and crafts projects we enjoyed working on together. One of my favorite activities was extracting the colors of beautiful flowers such as gladiolus. I remember my purple hands from these homemade dyes and the satisfaction of coloring my artwork with them.

Perhaps because I recall so little, an ordinary errand I was permitted to do takes on a special meaning. While Jews could still shop at Aryan-owned businesses, I was dispatched daily to the grocery store near the end of our block with an empty milk-pail. In exchange for a few *pfennigs*, the storekeeper would scoop out several ladles of fresh milk from her large aluminum vat, and I would carefully carry it home.

In preparation for the Sabbath, *Papi* would light the *Judenstern,* (Jewish Star) a six- pointed antique brass fixture which hung down from a link chain over a small round table. Each point of the lamp held some oil which gave off light throughout the night and by early Saturday morning it would have burned out.

I was 16 months old when this picture was taken in 1933

At dusk, *Mutti* lit the Sabbath candles while reciting the appropriate blessing and *Papi* would sanctify the wine with the *Kiddush*. Then he would break off a piece of the *challah,* sprinkle salt on it and chant the *motze,* the blessing over the bread. Our *Shabbat* meal would then be enjoyed in a festive atmosphere. The following evening when darkness signaled the conclusion of the Sabbath, *Papi* led us in the *Havdalah* ceremony, lighting a braided candle and then quenching its flame in a cup of wine. We passed the silver spice box around and everyone took a sniff as *Papi* wished everyone a *Gute Woche,* a good week.

I have a faint memory of *Das Gutes Zimmer,* the good room. This part of our apartment was beautifully appointed, in perfect order, ready when the doorbell rang. It was comfortable, but off-limits, and only used to receive and entertain guests. We enjoyed outings to sites of interest, playgrounds, parks, and the beach on the Rhein River. One intriguing excursion was to the medieval Heidelberg *Schloss* (Castle), where I was fascinated by the footprint, cast in concrete, of a man who escaped imprisonment by jumping over the high wall. I cannot recall whether the prisoner was a thief or prince, but the preserved evidence of his flight left an imprint on me, as well.

Of the few personal habits I recall, the most embarrassing was my thumb sucking. At almost nine years of age, I still went to sleep with my left thumb in my mouth and my right index finger twirling the blond curls on my forehead. Sometimes, I wonder whether the wavy hair of my adulthood was a direct consequence of this. As much as my parents tried, they could not break this habit. But on the first day of our deportation, when I began living with other children, I was miraculously able to fall asleep with both hands at my side. One exciting event occurred while I was too young to remember, but *Mutti* told me about it many times. She had tried to clean my nose with a swab of cotton before it was common practice to attach it to a stick. Somehow I inhaled the swab and had to be rushed to the hospital emergency room to have it extracted. After this incident I was allowed to walk around with a runny nose.

The Wetzler family in the mid 1920s: Grandma, Aunt Emmy, Aunt Nelly, Lilly (Mutti), Aunt Alice and Grandpa (Opa)

My Family and Early Childhood

Mutti was an accomplished violinist. I had always known of her talent and I heard her practice many times but I never suspected how far-reaching her reputation was. Some fifty years later while I was preparing for a pilgrimage to Europe, I happened to seek some information, and the voice on the other end of the phone immediately recognized the Weilheimer name. He asked: "Wasn't she the Cantor's daughter, the one who played the violin?" I was surprised that I had not known that *Mutti* performed with an orchestra at the concert hall of Mannheim, equivalent to New York's Carnegie Hall.

With my "tute" April 26, 1938

Admission to "German" schools was not available to Jewish children. Since *Mutti's* brother, Edgar, was not allowed to teach in an Aryan school, he became my teacher at the local Jewish school. The first day of school was always an exciting event. Traditionally, each child received a *"tute,"* a brightly decorated cone filled with candies and other goodies. Of course it was a glorious day, a milestone in a young life. I remember nothing else from that brief period, but I do suspect that Uncle Edgar gave me passing grades. After the Jewish schools were closed by the Nazis, my home schooling was exciting. I was *Opa's* (my maternal Grandfather's) favorite, actually his only, private student. *Opa* rolled up his sleeves and removed his ever-present necktie, and taught me to read and write as we sat at the fashionable raw wood table in the kitchen. *Oma* (Grandmother) was a good listener while discreetly attending to her kitchen chores. Sometimes she let me taste a morsel of that night's dinner. On an especially nice day *Opa* would open the door to a tiny balcony that overlooked the trees and plants in the back of the multi-leveled house at Wörthstrasse 10. I would take my lessons there, glad for the distractions.

Oma, me, Opa, Ernst in 1937

I remember the Passover holidays early in the Nazi era, although I have no recollection of how we conducted the *Seder* or who was in attendance. Perhaps I spent the entire eight-day holiday with my maternal grandparents. I vividly remember the daily ritual of accompanying *Opa* to a local café. We would always sit at the same outdoor table and his favorite waiter knew exactly what to serve him. He would bring a huge empty mug, almost as big as a cereal bowl, into which *Opa* meticulously stacked bite-sized pieces of matzo. As soon as *Opa* had coated the pile of matzo with a generous layer of sugar, the waiter poured strong aromatic black coffee over it. I believe his *Matzo Kaffee* was as much a tradition with him as reading the *Haggadah*. I was delighted to share his pleasure and I loved the bonding between us. I'm sure that I also had a treat each day at that café, but I cannot recall what it was.

Opa was a philanthropic man. He had a reputation as an "easy touch," unable to turn a poor stranger away from his door, and it was said that every Jewish traveler who needed aid made his way to *Opa's* apartment. I don't know if he dispensed only his own money or if the synagogue allocated discretionary funds for such handouts. I do know that he never disappointed anyone who genuinely sought his help, while he fiercely protected his assets from charlatans and pretenders. When a "blind man" made repeated visits, *Opa* dispatched one of his daughters to follow him to the end of the block and ask for the time of day. Without hesitation, he took out his pocket watch, confirming *Opa's* suspicion. On other occasions when a "Jewish" itinerant claimed to be *mittellos*, penniless, in the big city, *Opa* would test his truthfulness by asking the stranger to recite the *Sh'ma*, an important prayer with which any practicing Jew would be familiar.

Opa Salomon Wetzler in 1931

It was around 1936 when *Papi* placed me on the rattan seat mounted over the front wheel of his bicycle for an outing. We pedaled from Ludwigshafen over the Rheinbrucken

Be Happy, Be Free, Dance!

into Mannheim, where huge crowds had assembled along the railroad track anxiously awaiting the arrival of Germany's *Führer,* the iconic leader who vowed to cure all of the country's ills, restore its dignity and build an empire lasting a thousand years. In anticipation of seeing this savior, the animated spectators, many of them in a uniform of one sort or another, sang patriotic songs and shouted party slogans. I had no idea what Hitler represented. I only knew that he was the most important person on earth. His picture was everywhere; people intoned his name and saluted him constantly. It seemed that he was revered and followed by all Germans. *Papi* was less than enthusiastic and I had no idea why. He explained nothing to me when I gleefully asked him to hoist me on his shoulders so I could get a better glimpse of this idol. I watched with fascination as the train glided slowly over the tracks carrying men whose actions unbeknownst and incomprehensible to me, had already done immense damage, and were about to cause even greater tragic consequences. I must have blended right into the crowd for I had the perfect Aryan profile: blond, blue-eyed, fair skinned and possessing none of the so-called racial "defects" that the pseudo-science of eugenics attributed to Semitic people.

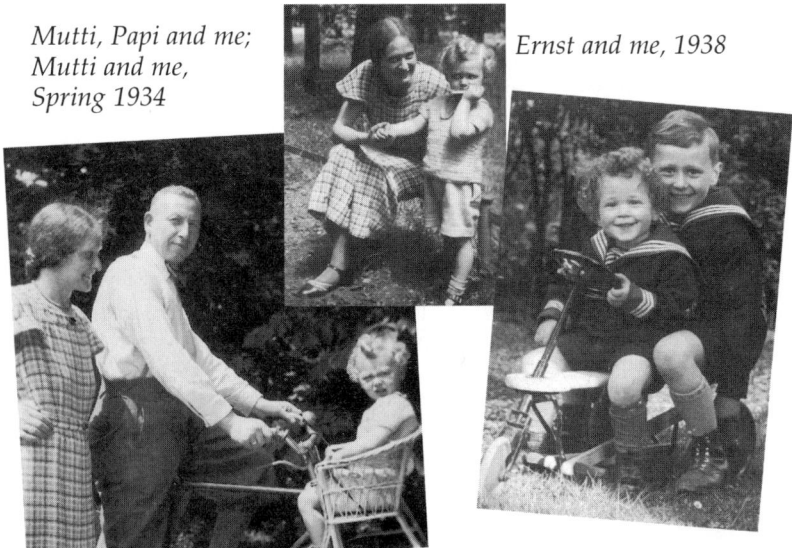

Mutti, Papi and me;
Mutti and me,
Spring 1934

Ernst and me, 1938

3. Kristallnacht and the Start of World War II

I was twelve days short of my seventh birthday on the night of November 9, 1938 – a time in a boy's life when he should be laughing and playing with children his age in a secure environment. It was not to be. The events of that infamous day exactly fifteen years after Hitler's unsuccessful attempt to seize power in the Munich Beer Hall *putsch* became etched in my mind forever. What was billed as a "spontaneous outburst of public furor" was actually a well-coordinated pogrom, deliberately orchestrated by the Nazi regime to be implemented at an opportune moment.

Herschel Grynszpan provided the spark for which the Nazis so eagerly awaited. This seventeen-year-old student in Paris had learned that his parents were among 17,000 Polish-born Jews deported from their home in Germany. Poland refused re-entry to former Jewish residents, including the Grynszpan family, who became refugees on a strip of land between the two countries. On November 7, having heard about his family's unbearable living conditions, young Herschel, in a rage, made his way to the German embassy in Paris, where he shot the first person he saw, who happened to be Ernst Von Rath, a junior embassy official. Von Rath died of his wounds two days later. The Gestapo used this "gift" to justify their assault against the entire German Jewish community.

Be Happy, Be Free, Dance!

Kristallnacht, often referred to as "The Night of Broken Glass," was the first violent Nazi mass action against German Jews. All the Jewish shops in Germany had been required to display a placard informing the public that the store was a *"Judisches Geschäft"* (Jewish business). This proclamation was hardly necessary since the windows were smeared with *Magnay David* (Stars of David) and graffiti that said *Jude* (Jew) in oil-based paint. Our family was awakened shortly before dawn by the sounds of destruction, shattering glass, and euphoric shouts by a sea of humanity gone berserk on the street below. Mobs of hooligans smashed the shops' interiors and looters felt free to claim whatever merchandise they desired. Piles of glass shards littered the sidewalks.

As frightening as those scenes were to this seven year old, they were eclipsed by the sight of the monsters who climbed three flights of stairs to the apartments where the store owners lived. They dragged out helpless, bewildered people, forcing everyone – including children and elderly parents – onto the street, wearing only their nightclothes on this cold November morning. The barbarians beat some people with clubs or whatever was in their hands. This image of bloodied children and their families will never leave me. Jews had no access to communications – no phones – we could not make contact with anyone.

Before we had a chance to think, mobs of thugs made their way through our cobblestone inner courtyard and stormed into our apartment. They wore no uniforms. They were unknown to us, just hordes of people stimulated by the Nazis, out of control with hatred for Jews. They grabbed my *Papi* and arrested him. We had no idea where he would be taken, or why, but there were no laws protecting Jews and no explanation was required. Days later, we heard that he was kept in a jail in Ludwigshafen overnight and shipped to Dachau concentration camp on November 11. Though he was eventually allowed to return, the child in me did not understand this. For many years, the memory of him being torn away from us haunted me. Did the Nazis let him kiss us good-by? Did he have time for an encouraging word; some assurance to his wife and two terrified young sons?

Taking hold of Ernst's and my hands, *Mutti* fled from the house. Together we walked the streets. This seemed aimless to me. What was *Mutti* thinking? Her husband of eight years had been so suddenly and violently snatched – in front of her and his two young children's eyes. No one knew if we would ever see him again. No good-byes, no final embrace. Wandering the streets of Ludwigshafen, the city of her birth, she must have wondered: Where were her friends? Where were the neighbors? Where were the people she had known all her life? What could she tell the two little frightened, bewildered children holding her hands so tightly? How could she reassure them? How could she possibly explain what they had just witnessed? If she said: *"wir sind Juden?"* "We are Jews." Would they have understood? Would anyone? We were forced to take the back streets as the main thoroughfares were off limits to Jews. *Papi* had two brothers who also lived in Ludwigshafen and that was *Mutti's* destination, but when we arrived there, we found out that the same scenario had taken place in their apartments. My uncles had been arrested and, as we later discovered, also shipped to Dachau. My bachelor Uncle Sigmund (Muni), and Ludwig who was married to Mathilde (Tilde) were the only Jewish tenants in their respective buildings. I recall Aunt Tilde telling us how she observed neighbors on the street pointing toward her window, probably telling the frenzied mob "That's where the Jews live." They were betrayed by people with whom they thought they had a good relationship, with whom they shared a cup of coffee not so long before.

We walked on, not grasping what was happening; naïvely thinking this action against the Jews was confined to local pockets of terror. Our new destination was the synagogue where *Opa* was the Cantor, where he chanted on so many

17

happy occasions, and was also the head of the religious school. Where would a Jew go when he could no longer find refuge in his home or business? As we approached the synagogue, we saw the flames from a distance. We could not determine whether the fire came from inside God's house of worship or the heap of sacred objects tossed and torched on the sidewalk. Ours was but one of approximately a thousand synagogues destroyed all over Germany on that day.

Ludwigshafen, until the years of the Third Reich, was a city known for harmony, tolerance and respect for all its citizens. From its founding, the population included an assimilated Jewish presence. A Hebrew congregation had been formed in 1854, and nine years later the fledgling membership acquired and converted a Christian church into the synagogue now in ruin. A monument to the seventeen young Jewish congregants killed in action while serving their country during the First World War stood in front of the entrance. The town's brave firemen had been my heroes and I was fascinated when their engines sped through the streets. To see them standing idly by their trucks that day, smugly satisfied that the fire from the synagogue would not spread to adjacent Aryan property, was very puzzling to me.

In German-Jewish tradition shortly after a newborn boy is given his Hebrew name at a *brit milah* (circumcision) ceremony, a wimpel is presented to the congregation to mark the occasion. This bit of folklore, created on a long strip of linen, functions as a torah binder: it protects the parchment and facilitates opening the torah at its proper place for the next reading. Our synagogue owned a very special wimpel. *Opa*, who was also a scribe, hand-embroidered my Hebrew name *Simon ben Mosche*, along with verses and scenes from bible stories on it. The long edges were beautifully finished with multi-colored yarn, in the same colors he used to illuminate this magnificent work of art. I cannot recall exactly when I realized that my very own wimpel, which, because of *Opa's* position was always kept on one of the scrolls, had been destroyed. It was a shock, more hurtful than the desecration of the synagogue itself. It carried my name, my identity. It was personal and it was plundered, as was the one bearing the name *Jakow ben Mosche*, which belonged to Ernst.

As we pondered what to do and where to go, we became aware of the chilly November weather. *Mutti* decided that we had to get back home to pick up sweaters since, in our rush to leave, we were not properly dressed. The sight that greeted us at the apartment has always remained embedded in my mind. Our home had again been violated and all our possessions were trashed. The intruders had evidently entered with sledgehammers and axes, and in an orgy of violence, they demolished the contents of our home. Every piece of furniture was knocked on its side and decimated into splinters. Dishes, knickknacks and life's little treasures and mementos lay in fragmented heaps. Everything we owned that had not previously been confiscated or stolen was smashed or destroyed. Clothes and linens, whatever they could not break, were dumped in the center of the rooms and liquids – whatever was in our home, inks, paint and molasses – was poured over them. I particularly remember the molasses since that unique smell has stayed with me throughout the years, and even now it instantly transplants me back to that very chaotic day. I don't recall what salvageable sweaters or jackets we took as my memory short-circuited at that point.

We headed towards the home of my *grosseltern*, my grandparents, in another section of the city and learned upon arrival that *Opa*, at 64 years of age, had also been arrested. He too was shipped to Dachau. My grandparents' neighbor, a Catholic woman, took us into hiding since no one knew what might happen next. I do not recall whether it was in her home or my grandparents' where we were confined in a small attic space for the next seven days and nights. I have no memory of how we spent the time nor do I recall any hygienic arrangements, but I do remember this wonderful lady bringing us food throughout our concealment.

The early concentration camps were not what they later became. Rather, they held mostly political prisoners and opponents of Hitler's policies. The thirty thousand Jews who were arrested following *Kristallnacht* were dispatched to Dachau, Buchenwald and Sachsenhausen with the intent to terrorize, degrade and dehumanize them. Their heads were shaved and they spent endless hours standing at attention in formation. Some were tortured and a few were killed but most were eventually released. About a thousand never returned home.

The Nazis had been simply waiting for some "justification" to assault the Jews and an excuse to implement the pre-conceived terror. Hitler recognized that this would be advantageous in minimizing possible foreign objections while spreading and intensifying anti-Semitism among the broad German public. The so-called "instinctive reaction" of the masses, having been manipulated to a boiling point, was actually a product of detailed planning and instructions on how to conduct the pogroms. Late in the evening of November 9, Heinrich Muller, the Chief of the Gestapo had sent a memo to all his offices around the country which stated:

*Actions against Jews, especially against their synagogues, will take place throughout the Reich shortly. They are not to be interfered with.

*Preparations are to be made for the arrest of about 20,000 to 30,000 Jews in the Reich. Above all, well-to-do Jews are to be selected. Detailed instructions will follow in the course of the night.

*Should Jews in possession of weapons be encountered in the course of the action, the sharpest measures are to be taken.

Reinhard Heydrich, the Chief of SS (Elite Guard/Security) issued his own orders "Concerning: Measures Against Jews in the Present Night" at 1:20 AM on November 10. The following excerpts are gleaned from his directive:

Kristallnacht and the Start of World War II

Only such measures should be taken as will not endanger German life or property (i.e. synagogues burning only if there is no danger from fire to the surroundings.)

Special care is to be taken that on business streets non-Jewish businesses are absolutely secured against damage.

Directly after the termination of the events of this night, as many Jews, especially the well-off ones, are to be arrested as can be accommodated in the available prison space. Above all, only healthy male Jews, not too old, are to be arrested. Contact is to be made with the appropriate camp regarding the quickest committal of the Jews to the camp.

The Reich Führer, SS, and Chief of the German police have ordered these measures.

Because this action was pre-organized, some Jews who had ties to individuals in the police or other civic departments were forewarned and they were able to leave their homes an hour or two before the "spontaneous" mob action took place. They were spared. We had no such connection.

***Opa* came home a week after his arrest** because the Nazis released some of the older prisoners first. We felt secure enough to leave the attic following his return and the absence of any further violent action. *Papi* came home five weeks after he was whisked away, having been freed because he and his four brothers had served Germany in the trenches during World War I. Each of them had been wounded, and one died in action in the Somme in 1916. (His name was Richard and I was named for him. Ernst was named after another of my father's brothers who died in 1908 of causes unknown to me.) The Weilheimer brothers were not unusual for their service to the Kaiser's army. Jews were very patriotic and supplied a disproportionate number of their young to Germany's military. Most served in combat and many were killed in action. They earned an extraordinary number of medals. Neither my father nor his brothers ever spoke of the war to me nor do I recall ever seeing any memorabilia or the medals they were awarded. Perhaps they had to return them or they were stolen. Eventually, my uncles and neighbors also came home but I have no idea how we coped and managed to return to our house. My memory of the following months has huge gaps.

This massive physical attack on the German Jewish community was the dawn of what we now label "The Holocaust," the beginning of the end of Jewish life in Europe. Six million people, guilty only of being born into our faith, were murdered. Millions of others were killed as well but only Jews were destined for total extinction. It was the first time in history that a people, a segment of humanity, were earmarked for total annihilation, without regard to political or geographical boundaries. *Kristallnacht* not only demonstrated the power of an evil government's prejudice but it clearly portrayed an indifferent, impotent world refusing to react to a crime against humanity.

Further insults and hardships ensued. The devastated Jewish community was collectively fined the outrageous sum of one billion marks (400 million 1938 dollars) for "stirring up the German population and causing this riot." Insurance companies were instructed to refuse all claims and, by intimidation and decree, Jews were forced to sell their remaining businesses to Aryans, at a fraction of their true value. We were refused normal service in Aryan-owned shops and all our economic activities ceased. Jewish cultural centers were closed and newspapers were banned from publishing. Those children who, by virtue of their fathers' World War I service in the German Army, still remained at public schools were now expelled. Our community could hardly sustain itself, so we created a system of trading services and goods amongst ourselves. *Papi* dealt in buttons and I can still visualize a bathtub, which he used as his "warehouse" full of sample cards and boxes. Our community was pauperized as those few assets which had not been confiscated became depleted. We were forced to beg from family, friends and neighbors.

Kristallnacht and the Start of World War II

Upon his release from Dachau, Papi was forced to file this "change of address" form listing his last address as Dachau Concentration Camp and his "new" address as Bismarkstrasse 15, where he had lived all his life.

Be Happy, Be Free, Dance!

November 9 and 10, 1938 was a reality check for Germany's Jews, the people who considered themselves "Germans first," who had once looked upon Hitler and his ilk as a troublesome but benign tumor that would be excised at the next election. Since the Nuremberg racial laws of 1935, many had tried to find another country that would accept them. Now they saw that their failure to find a sanctuary had become life-threatening. Fear turned into panic as they suddenly realized that this bold, unchallenged pogrom was the pivotal action leading in an irreversible direction. They would spend the following weeks and months lined up outside foreign consulates mostly in vain, trying to get on lists, under quotas to almost anywhere. The free world didn't want them. The absence of international reaction to *Kristallnacht* proved to the Nazis that the world did not care about the Jews. The silence was the grease that lubricated the German *Volk's* hate machine.

Hitler envisioned himself as the builder of an empire, first to encompass all of Europe, then the world. To do this he had totally disregarded and defied the terms of the Versailles treaty. He restored Germany's armament complex, rebuilt the military, and in 1936 he challenged the free world by ordering his troops into the Rheinland. His initial focus was on the Germanic countries where he anticipated little opposition. When his troops marched into Austria in early 1938, there was little resistance from its citizens, and or outcry from the world community. When the citizens of Vienna cheered and welcomed him, Hitler annexed Austria, followed by the ethnic German section of Czechoslovakia known as the Sudetenland. Prime Minister Neville Chamberlain of Great Britain, the spokesman for Western opposition to Nazi expansion, was desperate to avoid another war in Europe, so he succumbed to Hitler's "last demand" by agreeing to this takeover. It was a sell-out, a spineless appeasement to an evil empire. Chamberlain's "peace in our time" theory only encouraged further aggression and the onset of World War II.

Kristallnacht and the Start of World War II

The *Führer* honored his latest agreement as he did all other treaties: by invading one country after another. Hitler, still believing that he would have no meaningful opposition or intervention, ordered an attack on Poland for September 1, 1939. His *Luftwaffe* (Air Force) spearheaded the assault while ground forces decimated any opposition. Having promised to defend Poland against aggression, Great Britain and France declared war on Germany within two days. Poland could not stop the onslaught and was forced to capitulate in three weeks. This was Germany's first *Blitzkrieg* (lightning war) experiment and its success set the stage for further conquest in the east.

Soon thereafter, the British Royal Air Force and French bombers began a pattern of nightly air raids over Germany. Ludwigshafen, located beside the Rhein River, became a prime target because it had heavy industries, manufacturing facilities and a huge chemical industry geared to the Nazi war effort. Although Ludwigshafen was not always the primary destination of the bombers, air raid sirens sounded frequently and we ran to the damp shelter of our cellar. Our temporary refuge was a steel wire cage, a storage section in the subterraneous space reserved for *Juden* (Jews). There we experienced constant harassment, cursing, and name-calling, not because of any act we might have committed but purely because of who we were. "Dirty Jews – this entire war is because of you filthy vermin." Once we were locked in the cage for three days. I actually think ten year old Hitler youths did this, much to the pleasure and entertainment of their elders. I don't remember who finally released us or how we managed during our imprisonment. How frustrated and impotent my parents must have felt!

At the tender age of eight, I did not understand what was going on; childhood was a natural protector. I didn't even realize that the "bad guys" who did all this bombing, who brought on our discomfort in the bomb shelters and caused the hostile demonstrations against us, were actually the "good guys." At daybreak, I would survey the devastation. Our house was still completely intact, having suffered only some superficial pockmarks caused by the rain of spent anti-aircraft artillery. This curiosity gave birth to my first hobby, my inclination for collecting. I would search the neighborhood for pieces of shrapnel and soon amassed a respectable variety of jagged slivers of metal, including one which landed on our windowsill without breaking the glass. I was most interested in ones that appeared rusty or took on earthy tints from the gunpowder, nitrates and sulfurs. I preferred the small 2 to 4 inch fragments although I acquired some 8 to 10 inch pieces as well. I stored them in cigar boxes and cartons and – despite their threatening sharp edges – often took them out to admire their colors and shapes. Some were just too large and had to be left where they fell. I did not understand war and do not remember my parents talking to me about it. The whole subject of what was occurring in the sky and the visible destruction around us, together with the intensified hatred for Jews that plagued our everyday life, was taboo in our household. Nothing was explained either for fear that further violence might befall us or simply not to involve and frighten us children. It never occurred to me to raise any questions. As I became

The last photo of Mutti, Ernst and me in Germany, July 1940

aware of the hatred and harassment inflicted on us, I naively thought it was normal. "That's the way life is" and I had to learn to cope and survive like an animal in a jungle, always hunted by other animals.

In the spring of 1940, Germany's superior armored military machine directed its campaign towards Western Europe. In rapid succession, the Nazis occupied Norway, Denmark, The Netherlands, and Belgium. In June 1940, after a short ground war, France was forced to capitulate and sign an armistice agreement. The country was subsequently divided into two sections. The Nazis occupied the northern part while southern France was administered by the collaborator, Marshall Philippe Pétain. His "Vichy regime" (named after the French city where Pétain's headquarters were located) enthusiastically followed German orders, often exceeding the Nazis' demands. Thus, Jews who had been fortunate enough to escape Hitler's wrath by migrating to Western Europe were once more in his hands or those of his collaborators. Some local populations in conquered countries, accustomed to centuries of inbred anti-Semitism, facilitated laying the groundwork for an efficient genocide. The Germans could not have carried it out so easily without their help. On October 3, 1940, the Vichy government enacted anti-Semitic legislation known as *Status des Juifs*. The laws were in part the result of lingering sentiment from the Dreyfus case almost five decades earlier. French-born Jews were not persecuted at first, but Jews who had taken refuge there were soon rounded up and dispatched to transit camps.*

---

* While the Vichy government's complicity in anti-Semitic propaganda and action was deplorable, it must be noted that most of the Jews who survived in France were saved through the assistance of individuals and organizations in small towns and rural areas. Among the notable righteous people were the Huguenot Pastor André Trocmé, his village of Le Chambon sur Lignon which hid 5,000 Jews and Monseigneur Jules-Gèrard Saliège, the Archbishop of Toulouse who wrote a famous pastoral letter protesting against the deportation.

4. Deportation to Camp de Gurs

Once again the sanctuary of our home was violated. It was early on the morning of October 22, 1940, but this time is was not a mysterious mob. This time we knew. They were the notorious brutal Gestapo, the dreaded security police under whose authority Jews had been placed a couple of years before, and they wore the uniform intended to instill awe and fear. We were instructed to pack for immediate relocation. This order had been authorized by Hitler himself and was transmitted in utmost secrecy. If any Germans had been aware of the order and willing to risk warning their Jewish neighbors, they had few ways to do so since by this time Jews had been stripped of their radios and telephones.

The Gestapo informed us that we had one hour to pack and we could each take a single suitcase. One of the Gestapo sentries advised: "Take a wool blanket, warm clothing and enough food for several days." Later we learned that this action took place simultaneously in the entire Baden and Palatinate region in a drive to make this the first *Judenfrei* (Free of Jews) area inside Germany. To reduce the risk that non-Jewish neighbors might object to the deportation, every movie house had shown anti-Semitic propaganda films for weeks leading up to this day.

A lone guard watched us pack, coveting our possessions. Nazis hated Jews, but loved their treasures. Another posted himself at the front door. I don't know what my parents took with them. What would anyone take from the house where their family had lived for three generations? What would someone squeeze inside a single piece of luggage knowing there is no returning, no second chance to retrieve that which must be abandoned? An entire celebration of life — memorabilia and cherished possessions — had to be forsaken: photographs, family treasures, books, musical instruments, Judaica and many other irreplaceable heirlooms. Virtually everything of monetary value had already been confiscated, stolen or destroyed on *Kristallnacht* and later. Whatever might have miraculously escaped that fate must now be left behind. We could take no valuables and currency was limited to 100 Reischsmark (about $2.50) per person. They threatened to shoot us if we defied any of these conditions. Every bit of luggage space was preserved for what my parents considered essential, even as choices had to be quickly made. Obviously, there was no room for any children's games or prized trinkets, but a normal childhood had already been denied us.

Dear God, what did my parents have to endure? I only know for certain about one item that our family carried with us. Sixty years later, I learned that my father packed small photo albums in his suitcase that day: pictures of me and Ernst, with our parents and *Mutti's* family. Both of *Papi's* parents had died before I was born, but the little albums were his way to preserve a legacy for his sons: a glimpse of a more peaceful family life and relative normalcy. The Gestapo tried to persuade us to voluntarily leave the rest of our belongings to the Government. I don't know whether some people actually signed these prepared declarations, but we learned afterwards that our homes were sealed and all our possessions reverted to the Third Reich. Furniture and other contents were sold in public auctions several months later. Ironically, the property of "Dirty Jews" was coveted by those who "didn't know" or claimed "there was nothing we could have done."

Deportation to Camp de Gurs

Germans are always punctual. Within 60 minutes, police vans and trucks awaited us, already partially filled with other evicted Jews. As we were marched out of our house, the sentry at the door stuffed something in my five-year old brother's jacket. Ernst, frightened, quickly emptied his pocket, dropping half a salami on the steps. It was a short ride to an assembly place, the yard of a local school. Approximately two hundred Jews were already gathered there – mostly neighbors and friends from Ludwigshafen. A few hours later we were transported to the larger city of Mannheim, just across the Rhein River. There, at the railroad station, we were commanded to dismount rapidly and we found ourselves among approximately two thousand others, from infants to elders in their nineties. Some people had been forcibly evacuated from old age and nursing homes. The arrests had created a panic within the Jewish community and several people committed suicide before boarding the train.

We were reunited with our extended family: *Oma*, Uncles, Aunts, cousins of my parents and their close friends whom we also called "Aunt and Uncle." Only *Opa* was missing. He was in a hospital, afflicted with bladder cancer. Together with our parents, Ernst and I were loaded on one of the two trains that left Mannheim. These were not the cattle cars later used to ship Jews to the death camps. They were old passenger trains with seats ripped out and windows shuttered and sealed from the outside. People were crowded all over, some sitting on suitcases, others sitting on the floor or standing. The experience of that trip was such a shock that memories of most details are blocked. Some adults and children were crying in despair, and still more people committed suicide aboard these railroad cars. Others engaged in idle chatter. Perhaps they were hallucinating or unable to grasp the reality of our dilemma. In the excitement and urgency of their departure, had they remembered to pack essentials, taken a toothbrush, eyeglasses? Along our journey, the Nazis robbed many families of valuables they tried to bring with them as well as the meager 100 Deutchmark we had been allowed to take.

We were on that train for three days and three nights, not always moving. Europe is not that big. Often we were sidetracked for hours at a time. The only food or water we had during the first two days was what we had brought from home. On the third day, Friday October 25, we pulled into a train station. When the shutters which had kept us in dimness were opened, we immediately realized that we were in Southern France, Vichy France, in the City of Pau. The Nazi SS guards, having completed their mission, had disappeared and been replaced by Fascist Vichy soldiers. Much to our relief, there were civilians on the platform with rice and water for us. They were representatives from the American Friends Service Committee, a Quaker organization, who expressed their faith through humanitarian deeds. Our arrival on French soil was a complete surprise to the Vichy administration. Since the deportation had been carried out in secrecy, they first became aware of us when the trains roared in and this human cargo was dumped on them. But the Nazis merely wanted to cleanse Germany of its Jews; they didn't care what Vichy did with us. Vichy expressed some annoyance, and it did not fall on deaf ears; after all, the Nazis depended on their cooperation. So in order not to further offend them, no more Jews were sent to France.

After a short stopover we continued by train to the nearby town of Oloron St. Marie, a short distance north of the Pyrénées. We were then released from the confinement of three days journey to stand on the station platform in pouring rain. There was widespread confusion and anger as our very limited possessions were taken from us and piled onto a mountain of suitcases. We did not know if we would ever again see those few items, so randomly and quickly selected. What an unbelievable circumstance, we deportees from a "civilized" society found ourselves in.

Deportation to Camp de Gurs

We had so many questions. No one had answers and some no longer had the will to live. After hours of waiting in the rain, we were loaded onto an open truck which transported us to that days' destination. It was a pitiful sight. Old people and infants, the sick and helplessly lost souls all drained of strength and spirit.

Thus the Nazis began their ugly mission to rid the nation of its Jews; the first step in a process to free all of Europe and eventually the world of *untermenschen*. Hitler planned for Jews to be the first "race" destroyed in preparation for the "Thousand Year Reich." This was to be accomplished in stages: first by identification and isolation, then by humiliation, expropriation, deportation and finally extermination. Our community was thus at the point of expulsion by deportation, the intermediate solution, a holding pattern, to await the construction of the mass murder facilities.

Soaking wet, we arrived late in the afternoon at *Camp de Gurs* which was located just south of the town by the same name in the Basque region of the Basses Pyrénées near the Spanish border. Gurs was the largest of about ninety detention camps in France. It was originally built as a short-term facility for thousands of Spanish civilian refugees, volunteers in the International Brigade and defeated remnants of the Republican Army of the Spanish Civil War. It still held Spaniards, in separate compounds, while adding Poles, Jews and political prisoners from all over Europe. There were people who no longer belonged anywhere, persons without citizenship. The camp was located in what was known as "the free zone," but to Jews it would always be known as the "un-occupied zone." No one suspected that this place was merely an ante-room of death for most of us, a way station to hold us until the death camps in Poland were ready. We entered over a paved, nearly mile-long road, which ran through the center of the camp, separating it into two sections. At that time of the year, it rains in this region of France almost every day and the camp had inadequate drainage. The mud was deep and so sticky we had to remove our shoes because the suction made it almost impossible to walk in that quagmire. It was surely one of the most depressing sights my young eyes had ever seen. *Papi* and *Mutti* were unable to explain why we had to be here. Now years later, I cannot imagine the sense of failure they surely felt for not being able to protect their children.

The camp consisted of thirteen compounds called *îlots*, (Islands), each holding between 24 and 30 barracks into which sixty inmates could be stuffed. The various *îlots* were separated from one another by barbed wire, and sentries patrolled the perimeters reinforced by guard houses at the entrances. In addition, the whole camp was surrounded by more of this wire fortification. Men and women were quickly and efficiently separated and assigned to different compounds. Along with the other children too young to take care of themselves, I was relegated to a barrack in the women's section where *Mutti* could look after us. Some of us did not get our wet, damaged and partially plundered suitcases for a week after our arrival.

Camp de Gurs

Deportation to Camp de Gurs

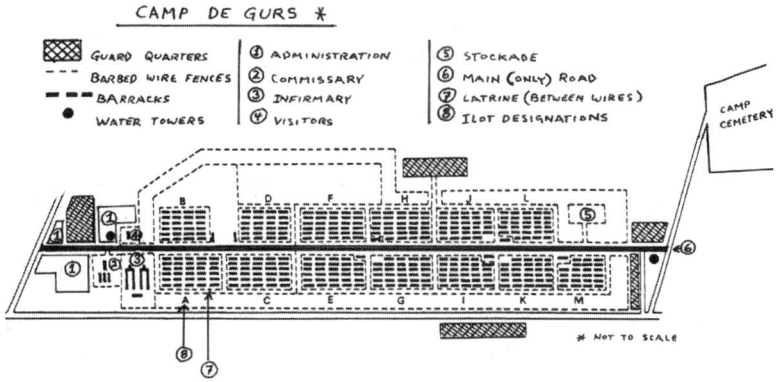

The flimsy barracks were no longer suitable for human habitation. They had been intended as temporary shelters, hastily constructed from wooden boards covered by a single sheet of tarpaper, and by now they had been totally neglected. They were filthy, with great gaps in the roofs and sides. Many boards had split and the tar paper was torn, allowing the rain to seep down and the wind to whistle through. The Spaniards had removed the wooden floorboards from the vacant barracks to which we were assigned, and used them to build crude furniture. So we had to sleep on the damp, bare ground. There were no mattresses, blankets or other necessities other than what we had brought in our suitcases. Instead of windows, hatch covers swung over openings on the sides, but most were not operable. Light and sufficient air could get in only when they were propped open with a stick. However this was not an issue, since the rain, extremely cold temperatures and lack of proper clothing left us little choice but to keep the sides completely closed despite the dank air and darkness. The little warmth had to be preserved. A single low-wattage light bulb was turned on for one hour each morning and afternoon leaving people at either end of the barrack in darkness. There was one pot-bellied stove but no wood to burn.

Sanitary conditions were crude. Rows of wash basins stood at the perimeter of each compound, near the barbed

35

wire. Once or twice daily, cold water would run through pipes into these tubs and one could wash in the open in full view of other inmates and guards. This was no place for modesty but people did their best to keep clean. As we washed our bodies, we would also rinse our clothing, and those who were lucky enough to have a vessel would carry water back to their barracks. Because of the limited time and wash stations, there were long lines and some unpleasant confrontations.

Primitive latrines were located alongside the barbed wire on the outer perimeter of the individual compounds. One had to go up five or six steps to reach these elevated platforms constructed of wooden planks with round holes cut into them, and steel drums below. We used these latrines for their intended purpose, doing what we had to, hoping the wind would not misdirect our leavings. We were given a limited amount of toilet paper to carry with us. There were small gauge tracks beneath these platforms and every two or three days a flatbed type of vehicle was pulled over them and a work detail – usually made up of teenaged boys or Spaniards – would replace the full drums with emptied ones. One can hardly describe the disgusting smells that permeated the camp. Before long almost every inmate was afflicted with dysentery. Some people disregarded hygienic common sense, especially during rain or darkness, and accomplished their needs behind the barracks.

Life was difficult at best in those first few weeks. Since the Vichy government was not informed about our arrival, they were unprepared to handle the logistics. Food was almost at starvation levels. A brown liquid, which was supposed to be coffee, was distributed each morning. Twice daily we were served what was known as soup, consisting of hot water with a few turnips and occasionally other vegetables such as carrots and beets and rarely, shreds of meat. A daily ration of bread so small that we needed to account for every crumb rounded out our miserly diet. Aid agencies later estimated that our daily food value was around 800 calories. Vichy allocated twelve francs a day for each inmate's ration, but it was well known that whatever the camp commander could save went into a special unaccountable fund. His name was Gruel (but many people called him "Cruel"). He was the biggest anti-Semite at the camp and only too happy to cooperate in any way possible with Vichy.* With every bit of food consumed, one would not think that rats could exist but they roamed freely throughout the camp day and night. We children were so afraid of them that at night, when we needed to relieve ourselves, we stepped but a few feet away from the barracks, or sometimes would wake several of our friends and with collective courage defy the rats and make it to the elevated seatless throne.

That was our initial view of *Camp de Gurs*. That is what greeted the more than 6,500 people expelled from the southwestern German provinces. The deportation had been accomplished by a ruse. As Jews were herded onto the trains, they were assured that they would be resettled outside Germany. Thus, amid gross confusion, disbelief and despair, there was hope: for deliverance, vain hope that world reaction would be forthcoming. But there were no outcries from the free world. Shortly after our arrival at Gurs, *Mutti* expressed her helplessness and frustration at our fate and her hope for a brighter future, resettlement and ultimate survival in a poem which she sent over to *Papi* at *îlot* B, Barrack 11. The translation follows:

---

* In December 1942, when the Nazis took over direct control of Gurs, Gruel, now answering to them, outdid the Germans by selecting and delivering more Jews for transport to the east, than were requested. This was beyond obeying orders. This was pure hatred and self-promotion.

Be Happy, Be Free, Dance!

Departure of the Jews from Germany

On October 22nd, at 7 in the morning
The Jews were chased out of Germany.
A historic day, oh terror, oh dread.
We Jews wandered out into the world,
Provided only with the bare necessities.
Where to, where to; there was no answer.
We wander out into the world.
The trains rolled through the dark night,
God's eyes watch out.
The night is over, the morning starts
Again we are surrounded by worries
But why brood and pretend?
We don't have anything more to lose.
They have stolen everything.
But whoever trusted in God remained strong.
They take us to our destination
Most everyone has gloomy thoughts
The destination, what is it like?
They put us in barracks.
Don't complain and don't cry.
The sun will soon shine for us also.
Seven lean years have passed
From '33 - '40, it is of no consequence.
Now there will be seven fruitful years.
They still didn't steal our faith.
God wanted to free us from servitude.
We should not regret being here.
In a few weeks we will continue on.
Keep your head high and be cheerful.
Never was the Jew annihilated
Despite his enemies' greatest wish.
Whoever digs a hole for others
He himself will not live long.

Deportation to Camp de Gurs

Auszug der Juden aus Deutschland.

Am 22. Oktober, morgens um fünfen
wurden wir Juden aus Deutschland vertrieben.
Ein historischer Tag, ich denken ich daraus
Wir Juden wandern in den Wald hinaus.

Mit dem Notwendigsten versehen,
Mußten wir von dannen gehen.
Wohin, wohin, die Antwort blieb uns,
Wir wandern in den Wald hinaus.

Die Züge rollten durch finstere Nacht
Das Auge öfters darüber wacht.
Der Nacht wich, es tagt, es wird Morgen,
Wieder umgeben uns dieselben Sorgen.
Wozu noch das Grübeln und Sinnieren an?
Wir haben doch nichts mehr zu verlieren!
Man hat uns Alles schon geraubt,
Doch stark bleibt, wer an Gott geglaubt.
Zu unserm Ziel man schickt uns hin,
Die Meisten mit betrübtem Sinn
Das Ziel weiß man noch ab dem nach aus?
Man hat uns nur Lug verkauft uns.
Ihr müßt nicht klagen & nicht weinen
Auch uns wird bald die Sonne scheinen.
Dieben unserer besten Jahre sind vorbei,
Von 33—40 ab ist nicht einerlei.
Dieben kriegsbare Jahre werden nie kommen
Man hat uns die Ehre auch nicht genommen.
Aus der Knechtschaft wollt uns Gott befreien,
Daß wir frei sind, sollen wir nicht bereuen.
In einigen Wochen sind wir weiter,
Hier den Kopf hoch und immer heiter
Nie ist Jude untergegangen
Trotz seiner Feinde größten Verlangen,
Wer Anderm eine Grube gräbt
Der selber nicht mehr lange lebt.

L.W.

Be Happy, Be Free, Dance!

Reich Jews Sent to South France, 10,000 Reported Put into Camps

Deportations From Palatinate and Baden, Agencies Here Learn – American Workers Seek to Ease the Group's Acute Needs

The forced evacuation in the last two weeks of more than 10,000 Jews from the southwest German Provinces of Baden and the Palatinate and their internment in concentration camps in southern, unoccupied France, has been reported to agencies here. The situation has brought new and additional problems to the organizations engaged in helping refugees in Germany, France and other European countries, it was stated yesterday.

Cabled appeals for immediate assistance said the relief problem was most acute at Camp de Gurs, near the Spanish frontier in southern France. About 9,000 persons, in age from six months to 98 years, have been sent there by the Germans from the Palatinate, Baden and near-by regions. Most of the refugees in this camp were said to be women and children.

Many men were sent to Camp Saint Cyprien in the same territory while other men, women and children totaling another 10,000 were sent to Camps Vernet and De Milles, also near the Spanish border in unoccupied French territory.

The French had been forced by the Germans to assume responsibility and care for these refugees, it was stated, and reports received here indicated that such aid was at a minimum. It was noted that the French authorities had a problem caring for their own nationals because of scarcities in necessities of life.

Deportation Reported as Hasty

The Jews reported sent out of the Southwest German Provinces were permitted to take only a minimum of money and clothing, amounting for an individual at the most to $2.50 and very little beyond the clothes they wore.

In the majority of instances those affected by the evacuation orders had less than half an hour to leave their homes. Much suffering resulted when families were forced to separate, the men going to one concentration camp and the women and children to another.

At Camp de Gurs the refugees, it was said, were forced to live in small wooden barracks with not enough water and practically without food supply. The barracks had been used by Spanish Republican refugees and when the Jewish refugees arrived

Deportation to Camp de Gurs

the buildings were in need of repair.

A number of the refugees had obtained visas to come to the United States, but ... the Germans ... blocked the prospective trips.

These particular refugees were said to have been told they would have to obtain new visas, new affidavits and go again through all the routine they had already accomplished before they could start for the United States or South American countries. As they were without funds, it was virtually impossible for them to get the necessary documents and money.

Joint Committee Attempting Aid

A coordinating committee consisting of representatives from the American Red Cross, the Quakers and the Joint Distribution Committee, handling relief for the Jews, has been visiting the camps and extending whatever aid it could. Actual relief work has been administered under the supervision of the Quakers.

Spokesmen for the relief agencies explained that it is possible for relatives and friends to forward from this country through proper channels $50 a month for each individual in a concentration camp. Some of the French residents near the camps were reported as willing to accept as paying guests those who could provide that amount for maintenance.

In many instances, however, these French were reported to be asking for a single payment for twelve months in advance. Very few refugees could meet these terms, because existing regulations here limit the amount they may receive from abroad to $50 monthly to an individual. An attempt would be made, it was stated, to have the United States Government make this regulation more elastic.

The relief agencies here also voiced the hope that some plan might be worked out by the State Department whereby it will be easier for those in the concentration camps to obtain the necessary documents and visas.

Some of the refugees now in the Southern French provinces who wanted to come to this country were said to have submitted their affidavits and other documents to the United States Consul at Stuttgart. These papers were not released by the consulate and therefore any applications for visas from Southern France must be made to the United States Consul at Marseille, it was stated. It was suggested that transfer of the applications from the Stuttgart Consulate to the one at Marseille would facilitate matters.

The New York Times,
early November **1940**

Be Happy, Be Free, Dance!

Early in November 1940, shortly after our arrival in Gurs, *Mutti* wrote to her sisters and brothers-in-law in America:

Dear brothers and sisters!

We have been here almost two weeks, except for our dear father. It was not possible to transport him. He had to stay in the hospital because of his bladder problem. We thought he might be here, but we learned that he had been taken to St. Teresa's Hospital in Mannheim. It is so desperately sad to be separated just at this time. Send the immigration papers to Mannheim at once. It might just work, even if his number has not come up yet. Did you send our papers to Marseille? Please do it at once so that we can get away. Ask Aunt Hedwig for Uncle Joseph's address (Limoges) and ask him to take us in until we can move elsewhere. You will have to finance it with Aunt Hedwig, Uncle Emil and Alfred Weilheimer. We are agreeable to anything. It is cold at night here and very hot during the day. Mother and I and the children do not have the least bit of clothing suitable for this heat. We left with only our winter garments, not a single summer item. Dreadful, everything. We all packed without using our heads, as you can imagine, and we left the best things behind. But we are not in a position to change anything and the most important thing is that we stay healthy. I have a lot of nerve pain, rheumatism and arthritis and it is absolutely vital that we get away from here. If only we had reservations for five ship's berths we could leave immediately. Has Roosevelt not made any financial help available for us? Please contact all committees and relatives and send us passages if you want to see us again as healthy beings. You must do it at once. Poor mother and her blood pressure! There are people here who have received telegrams from the U.S. that their ship's passage is on the way. So, rescue us!

Warmest kisses, your loving Lilly.

Three months after our deportation to Gurs, *Opa* sent a letter from the hospital in Mannheim to his son-in-law, my Uncle Kurt in the USA. *Mutti* had gotten sick and *Opa* was concerned because she had a low immigration number which had not yet been called. He said it was possible for him to travel to Gurs but he had been advised not to do so. He would stay in Mannheim, although it was no longer legal. *Opa* was free to send mail to America because the two countries were not yet at war. But he could not write to us at Gurs since France (even though the government was by then collaborating with the Nazis), was considered Germany's enemy. His letter is in the Appendix, page 169.

People died every day, particularly the very young who could not be protected and the elderly who could not adapt to this terrible depraved life. (The number of older people in the camp was disproportionately high because most pensioners had been unwilling or unable to emigrate from Germany.) Most of the Jews had come from a comfortable upper or middle class life style; no one was accustomed to the physical demands of living in the open air, and it had been a particularly harsh winter. Many had an intense desire to die. Some were chronically sick and feeble minded. They lay around apathetically, often refusing food and waiting for the end. Having endured such a long chain of trials, their lives were beginning to unravel and crumble. We were plagued by many annoyances. No one escaped the wrath of lice, fleas and bedbugs. Elderly people who tried to make their way to the latrines during the night sometimes collapsed in the mud and were found frozen at daybreak as temperatures fell to 10 - 15 degrees Fahrenheit. We often saw an open truck on the paved road, with the feet of dead bodies protruding over the tailgate.

It was pathetic to see these old people die. Many had adult children who had emigrated to the United States, England or Palestine during the late nineteen thirties, and who had been trying in vain to send for them. Now, alone in dirt and misery, often among total strangers, they reached their ultimate destination. During the first few months, about twenty people would succumb to the lure of death every day, a rate which could have eliminated the whole German Jewish camp population in less than a year. Although it was probably the worst concentration camp in Vichy controlled France, at the outset none of the Gurs inmates could possibly have envisioned the death of so many of their group – not from mass executions but due to the brutality, widespread disease, the elements and the breakdown of the will to endure these hardships.

The Spaniards began to sell us the boards that they had previously removed from the barrack floors and with the aid of wire from which the threatening barbs had been clipped, we built makeshift beds. The Vichy authorities had managed to obtain straw for us to sleep on and then they provided us with sacks to stuff so that we had "mattresses." It turned out that the straw was rotten and infested with vermin. The Spanish population at Gurs was very different from ours. They had been there for a much longer period of time and most came voluntarily to escape the fascist dictator Franco. They shared our camp, but because some had briefly served in the French Army they had a few special privileges. Naturally, their relationship with the guards was very different from ours. They arranged for us to make short evening visits to their well-stocked canteens where they traded foodstuffs for items we smuggled out of Germany. No doubt they bribed the Vichy guards who enjoyed their "humanitarian" conduct.

Those first few weeks were long and intolerable. There were no tables or chairs. We children had no toys nor could we entertain ourselves or play. The women had nothing much to occupy their time. They had no sewing material and aside from washing clothes, no household chores. The atmosphere was one of helplessness and frustration. Initially, when families were separated, we could not visit our loved ones in other *îlots*. Then opportunities to meet became more common, as individuals could visit the sick in infirmaries and groups could mingle at funerals on the cemetery grounds. Eventually a pitiful number of inter-compound visitation passes were issued. Inmates had to wait weeks for their turn. Sometimes, when they finally received a pass, they discovered upon arrival that their spouses had died.

The food situation improved somewhat. Because some deportees smuggled in wristwatches, earrings or other jewelry, they were able to organize a black market with the help of the Spaniards. This was eventually augmented by small amounts of money that relatives were able to send through organizations actively trying to alleviate the suffering. Some of us even obtained parcels with clothing and an occasional chocolate bar or canned goods, such as sardines. One could barter for flour, rice, noodles and cooking fats. At one point, we set up our own canteen, where we could purchase an egg or flour or other things not seen since our deportation. Though undernourished, many of us stayed relatively healthy because we could incorporate a few treats in the otherwise meager diet. But this canteen did not last long because it quickly became impossible to stock it.

Papi lighting Chanukah candles, Gurs, 1941

It was important for the inmates to maintain some semblance of order, some humanity, and some organization in their lives. Each barrack elected a chief and the council of barrack chiefs chose a "Chief of *îlot*." Even with such limited authority, this governing body definitely helped raise morale. The council had the energy and courage to provide for stimulating diversions in their *îlots*, including religious services on Friday nights and Saturdays for Jews, and

Sunday church services for those of the Catholic and Protestant faiths. The camp held many intellectuals and cultured people who offered lectures in history, philosophy and other topics of interest; anything to keep one's mind from atrophying. We were motivated to start entertainment groups, to maintain some sort of humor and create an informal "school" for the young. A sense of caring for one another permeated the camp; the communion of suffering created a touching solidarity. But the women at Gurs suffered disproportionately. They received less food, walked around aimlessly in torn clothing and were subjected to rough guards who had sole supervision over them. Thus, though the inmates worked hard to keep a semblance of human dignity, the habitual surveillance and harsh life took a particularly heavy toll on the female population. The camp cemetery which had been established at the time of the Spaniards' arrival sadly increased in size by almost 1,000 graves during the first three months of the German-Jewish presence. Because of the shortage of lumber, it was necessary to demolish an unused barrack to build coffins. It was not possible to hide these activities and frequent funerals from us children.

Children of my age adapted amazingly well to the miseries of camp life. Most sentries were not hostile towards us and at times they even appeared to be compassionate. We started hanging around their guardhouses and communicating without the use of language. They allowed us to maintain the fires which they continuously kept burning to warm their hands and feet; occasionally rewarding us with a piece of bread from their own rations. Sometimes they looked away, and aware of our destination, permitted us to claw through the mud beneath the barbed wire to visit our fathers. One time, the wire snapped and gashed my right hand and kneecap. The scars remained into my early adulthood.

Deportation to Camp de Gurs

Our parents did everything possible to reassure us and to persuade us that our confinement would be temporary. I do not recall any time that *Papi* or *Mutti* displayed any serious concern about our family's well being. I believe that they, along with most adult inmates, truly envisioned their eventual resettlement somewhere in a Jewish community, free from Hitler's ever extending reaches. The Vichy camp administrators and guards encouraged this feeling as it gave them better control of the population. In the early days behind barbed wire, no one tried to escape although it would not have been difficult. There was a greater fear of the risks outside the camp than within its confines. To the south were the treacherous Pyrénées with their frozen crests, and beyond lay Spain, a country which expelled its Jewish citizens back in 1492. Ruled by the dictator, Franco, Spain was Hitler's benign ally, having been helped in its Civil War by the Nazis who used that conflict to train their own air force and test their weaponry. Escape from Gurs into the French countryside did not seem wise. Camp inmates had no access to false identification cards which would have helped if they were apprehended by the Vichy collaborators who were under orders to turn them over to the Nazis in the occupied northern zone. We had not yet heard of Auschwitz. Gurs was our Satan, the one we knew and lived with, and preferred to the many unfamiliar Satans outside the barbed wire enclosure.

We waited for that illusive freedom, the resettlement in that fairy tale Jewish colony while singing the following song:

In den Bas-Pyrénéen steht ein ort wo barraken nur stehen, kein baum wachts dort. Dort kummt nur der hieneim den kein recht hatt auf platz betratt den trennung von der welt fon ein stacheldrat.

(In the Bas-Pyrénées there is a place where only barracks stand, no tree grows there. Only those who have no right to be in this world get sent there and whoever is confined to this space is separated from the world by barbed wire.)

17.4.41. April

Meine lieben Kinderchen!

Mit Deinem lieben Brief, mein lieber Richardle, habe ich mich sehr gefreut und ich danke Dir sehr für Deine Nachricht. Dass Du und mein liebes Ernstele gesund seid höre ich immer gerne und ich bete täglich zu Gott, dass er Euch gesund erhalten möge. Hoffentlich wird es nicht allzulange wo die liebe Mutti, Du und Ernstele wieder beisammen sind, dann wollen wir alles wieder nachholen. Die liebe Mutti hat immer noch viel Schmerzen und liegt noch in der Infirmerie, ich hoffe jedoch, dass es bald besser wird. Mir selbst geht es gut, das heisst, ich bin gesund. Wenn Du Deinem Briefe selbst, mein liebes Kind, Ich freue mich immer, wenn Du nach unserer lieben Mutti's Ergehen fragst, denn dies beweist mir immer Deine xxxxxxxxxx Anhänglichkeit. Ich schicke Dir anbei die gewünschten Briefmarken, nächste Woche schicke ich Dir wieder, das heisst ich schicke Dir gleich die adressierten Couverts mit. Dass bei Euch gutes Wetter ist, ist sehr schön, bei uns ist es eben auch warm. Da könnt Ihr doch sicher Euch viel im Freien bewegen und spielen. Vielen Dank für die Grüsse von lieb Manfred und Hans, grüsse dieselben bitte wieder. Herr Lehrer Stahl ist noch hier, er ist aber krank und liegt in der Infirmerie. Ich konnte daher Deine xxxxxx xxxxx xxx. Jedenfalls ist es sehr nett von Dir, dass Du daran dachtest. Herr Lehrer Ehrlacher ist nicht mehr hier, er kam vor einigen Tagen nach La Milles. Von der lieben Oma kam heute ein Brief an. Sie ist gesund und sie erwartet anscheinend einen Brief von Dir. Kauft Euch nur ab und zu etwas Obst, Dattel und Birne. Wenn Ihr kein Geld habt so schreibe mir bitte, dann schicke ich Euch dann etwas. Die Grüsse an die Leute der Baracke 11 habe ich ausgerichtet. Die Leute danken Dir bestens und sind nicht mehr bei uns, sie kamen nach Recebedou. Die Elikanns sind nicht mehr als ich noch meine Ämter habe. Ja die lieben Richardle, Du fragst? Ich habe die Leitung des Gottesdienstes übernommen, da Herr Oppenheimer von hier weg kam. Ausserdem bin ich mit in der Leitung für die Massenversorgung des Flots und für die Brachküche und Kost und so noch vieles andere. Die Kinderführung in die Speiseanstalt habe ich nicht mehr da keine Kinder mehr hier sind. Lieber Richard, es war sehr nett von Dir, dass Du uns zu unserem Geburtstage gratuliert hast. Ich hatte gestern, die liebe Mutti hat am 24.4. Ich danke Dir für Deine Aufmerksamkeit. Ich war bei der lieben Mutti und wir haben schöne Stunden zusammen verlebt, hoffentlich sind wir am nächsten Geburtstage wieder alle gesund

5. La Maison des Pupilles

In due time, various organizations such as *Secours Swiss*, the YMCA, Protestant social workers, the Unitarian Service Committee, Jewish social workers and of course, the Quakers, brought in food, materials, musical instruments, tools, and books which contributed powerfully to raising our spirits. Of the numerous organizations that had access to the Camp, the Quakers were the most active because of a unique relationship with the Germans. After Germany's defeat in the First World War, this non-political, pacifist humanitarian Christian group, properly known as the American Friends Service Committee, established soup kitchens and distribution centers to assist the needy in Germany. This deed was not forgotten and the Quakers were initially allowed to operate at the camp without administrative interference.

Immediately after our arrival, the Quakers in Toulouse sent social workers to *Camp de Gurs*. They were assigned a barrack to use as a supplementary kitchen and distribution center, from which they were able to dole out milk for infants and additional food for the adult population. They also issued warm clothing, underwear and socks. Though everything was still in extremely short supply, their contributions made a huge difference in maintaining our strength and sense of well-being. (A 1941 letter describing the activities of the American Friends Service Committee, sent from their Toulouse office to their Philadelphia headquarters can be found on page 170.) The

Be Happy, Be Free, Dance!

Quakers knew of an orphanage in the southern French town of Aspet, about 65 miles south of Toulouse near St. Gaudens in Haute-Garonne. *La Maison des Pupilles de la Nation* was barely half filled yet it suffered a chronic shortage of rations for its young French residents who had been orphaned during the brief period of their country's participation in the war, or abandoned by a surviving parent, unable to cope.

Operating out of their field office in Toulouse, it took four months for the Quakers to negotiate arrangements to transfer fifty children from *Camp de Gurs* to fill the vacant beds at the orphanage. The Quakers pledged to supplement the rations of the French orphans and to provide food for the camp children as well. Of course, it was not easy to persuade the parents at *Camp de Gurs* to make the painful decision to permit their children to leave, as they could not imagine the future nor benefit from our hindsight. Most inmates clung to the hope that their family would ultimately re-locate to an all-Jewish community, such as the French colony of Madagascar. Parents were legitimately hesitant and fearful about further separations, and some children refused to part from them. A few children experienced deep feelings of deprivation and abandonment, while others worried that they were a burden, no longer loved, no longer wanted. In reality, it took great courage, foresight and selflessness for parents to send their children off alone into a hostile world so unforgiving to Jews.

Final arrangements were made by the Quakers acting in concert with *Oeuvre de Secours aux Enfants* or OSE, a far-sighted Jewish organization which anticipated the deteriorating circumstances for the inmates of Gurs. Together they persuaded the local Vichy authorities to allow the fifty children to leave their barbed wire confinement. In eight cases, either the parents or the children had second thoughts and changed their minds about separating. Hastily only six replacements were found. Thus, forty-eight boys and girls from about five to thirteen years of age were released from the camp at the end of February 1941. *Mutti* had been ill by this time, so my parents had lobbied the Quaker/OSE committee to include Ernst and me. They had no foresight or intuition of things to come; but they understood *Mutti's* health situation and the camp's harsh life and they believed that a children's home, no matter how strained during wartime, was still a better atmosphere. I know they truly thought a reunion would not be far off. Since our departure from the camp was legal, the Vichy authorities never challenged our trip. An OSE representative named Andrée Salomon, along with a young couple whose name was Cohen, accompanied us to the orphanage. After delivering us to our destination, the three adults had to take flight as their trip was unauthorized, made without the required documents. Later on they were able to obtain papers and visit us periodically. They were our intermediaries, confidants and advocates, and they reported back to our families in Gurs

It was a cold rainy day when we said good-bye to our parents, each of whom was reluctant to part from their children. We did not know then that in almost every case, it was a final parting. Not one of our parents would survive the Holocaust. Forty-eight children would soon be orphaned.

Although it was only a short distance to Aspet, wartime movement was not easy. We traveled in trucks to the railroad station at Oloron St. Marie, by train to St. Gaudens, and then by bus to *La Maison des Pupilles*. We arrived late at night, hungry, dirty, bewildered and frightened. We had never been away from our parents before and couldn't understand exactly where we were or why. Instructions were given in French, a language we could not speak or understand. Before we were fed some meager rations, we had to undress, relegate our clothing to the disinfecting pile and take showers in the basement of the main building. I had never heard of a shower, as we only had bathtubs in our house in Germany and wash basins in Gurs. Boys and girls showered together that first night, giving me my first close-up opportunity to study the difference in anatomy. Because of the lice and illnesses we carried, there was a thirty day quarantine period during which we could only participate in activities with our own group. We felt abandoned, lonely and scared. The French children added to our misery, taunting us, calling us *Boches,* or *Krauts,* a reference to Nazis. This was very painful but quite understandable since their country had just been defeated and occupied by the Nazis and their Vichy puppets. Some of their relatives had been in the French army and others, no doubt, were in the resistance. We spoke only German and they had no idea of our background, nor could they differentiate between the Nazi conquerors and their victims. There were many fights, until our group established its "turf" and subsequently we had an amicable relationship with the French children. Our lack of French and the administrator's inability to communicate with us in German posed a problem. The Quakers sent a young woman to be our translator and advocate. Her name was Alice Resch (later Synnestvedt) and she became our "Den Mother."

Alice, the 32-year-old daughter of Norwegian parents, was born in Chicago while her father was working for Westinghouse Corporation. At the age of five, the family returned to Norway where she had an idyllic childhood. After completing school there, she pursued higher education in Germany, graduating from the University of Heidelberg. Somewhat of a rebel and a feminist, ahead of her time, she went to France and studied nursing. During the Spanish Civil War, she volunteered with the American Friends Service Committee office in Toulouse, and spent time at *Camp de Gurs.* She spoke Norwegian, German, English and French fluently and had a working knowledge of other tongues. Alice was a "take charge"

La Maison des Pupilles

woman who quickly won our trust. There were no private rooms in the orphanage, so she moved into the dorm with us. She put up a curtain to separate herself from the children and because he was one of the youngest, chose my brother, Ernst, to sleep in the bed nearest to her.

The headmaster, Monsieur Couvot, was a fair man but a strict disciplinarian, punishing and hitting children for minor infractions, like crying or wetting their beds at night. Many children were assigned responsibilities or

Alice Resch Synnestvedt, our "Angel of Aspet"

chores. My job was to shepherd the orphanage's flock of thirty sheep. Accompanied by an old dog, whose name I cannot recall, I led my flock over the meadows towards the foothills of the Pyrénées early each morning. One evening, halfway back to the pens, I counted my charges and came up with twenty-nine. Panicky and fearful of Monsieur Couvot, this nine-and-a-half year old shepherd left the old dog in charge and retraced his steps. Sheep number thirty was docily grazing several hundred yards back. Returning to where I left the flock, I only found the dog, asleep. Another panic attack, some pleading with a now half-awake dog and we were off to search for the twenty-nine renegades. Somehow we all came together and no one knew of my anxiety that day.

Be Happy, Be Free, Dance!

Food was limited but adequate considering where we had come from. Sometimes we even could dip our morsels of bread into olive oil. I never forgot this incredible treat. The older children occasionally had some red wine diluted with water. Our recent experiences had made us fearful about whether there would be any food for tomorrow, so we routinely squirreled away bread, fruit or whatever we could in case we might not get anything the next day. Some of us saved food for our parents who kept sending us reassuring letters saying that they expected to get out of the camp and visit us soon. None of them ever obtained passes to visit but a few of the older boys were able to get back to Gurs for a day or two and deliver what we had hoarded for them.

We often took hikes in the countryside and would beg farmers for apples, slices of bread or anything edible. Along the way, we gathered and ate nuts that had fallen from the trees. Some of the boys would play cards using crumbs of bread for chips. We were hungry, as growing children are, lacking basic vitamins and a healthy diet, but no longer starving. Miraculously, we had regained the weight lost during our brief internment behind the barbed wire in Gurs. Most of us were in relatively good health but susceptible to illnesses associated with the lack of a proper diet and living among so many children. I can't recall what trained medical staff there was, but somehow all of

Jewish children at La Maison des Pupilles, Aspet, Spring 1942
Ernst is first at the left; I'm fifth.

La Maison des Pupilles

us did O.K. One time, Ernst developed a wheezing sound in his chest and they placed heated sandbags on him to help his breathing. But the sand was too hot. He was quite burned and the blisters scarred his skin for a long time. Some Jewish farmers and landowners lived in the countryside nearby, and every weekend several of us were invited to spend the day and share a meal at their tables. I don't know who these strangers were but I never stopped thinking of them and the great comfort they gave us just when we needed it. Alice Resch was always there for us until we settled into a stable existence. Then she left for other rescue missions, but she periodically came back to check on us and make sure things were all right.

At least we were able to exchange letters with our parents and they could send packages to us from Gurs. Papi and Mutti wrote to us on March 14, 1941

Good Shabbos, My Dear Children,

Oma has forwarded the letter which you wrote for all of us. We take much pleasure with it and seeing that you are healthy and have adjusted well. Hopefully you also have enough to eat. Take care of yourselves, stay healthy, behave and learn nicely. Above all, write whenever you can in detail as it is our greatest pleasure to receive mail from you. In my next letter I will again send you postage stamps. If you need anything else feel free to write and I will mail it to you. I located a pair of training pants for Ernstele and will send it at the next opportunity. What do you do all day long? Stay well and be hearty.

Your loving, Papi

My Dear Boys,

Many thanks for your letter but I ask of you dear Richardle, the next time write it all by yourself even if you make mistakes. Enjoy playing, be happy and merry. Eat whatever you get so you will have enough. I feel better.

Greetings, your loving Mutti

Eventually, arrangements were made for us to attend a public school in Aspet where we learned to speak, read and write French, something I quickly and totally forgot. Jewish teachers from neighboring communities also conducted religious classes and led Friday evening services at the orphanage. The services were followed by *Oneg Shabbat* gatherings where anyone who had received a package of sweets or other food during the week shared their goodies with the others. These packages came from distant and sometimes unknown relatives who lived in France, Portugal and other countries who learned of our whereabouts from our parents. Moritz and Friedel Wildstrom, a German-Jewish refugee couple who lived near the orphanage, visited frequently to help us celebrate birthdays and holidays. Their nearness gave us great comfort and reassurance.

Unable to comprehend the abyss of human behavior in a world from which we were never far removed, we did lose ourselves in some measure of happiness. These were the best of times in the worst of times. After all, children have a basic human right to be children. We were constantly aware of our circumstances and the plight of our parents but everyone encouraged us to have hope and live as normally as possible. We participated in sports, played tennis and formed a soccer team. We never saw a game board or children's toys, but we found companionship within our group. The only game I remember playing – being addicted to – was marbles. We would create a labyrinth in the sand, complete with banks on both sides. We took turns trying to be the first to reach the finish line. My right thumb was always ready to propel the marble out of the crook of my index finger as far as I would dare, so as to avoid shooting over the banks. I was quite good at it and even prouder of possessing my very own marble.

La Maison des Pupilles

March 25, 1941

My Dear Children,

We are very pleased with your letter of 3/16. We see from it that you are healthy and well settled. Always behave, be obedient and learn well. Most of all, remain healthy and in good spirits. I would be very pleased if you would write by yourself Richardle and not let other boys write for you. Let us know everything in detail as we are all very interested in what you and Ernstele do. Are you going to school yet? Several days ago I sent you a parcel with articles of clothing for Ernstele and for both of you zwieback and chocolate. Hopefully it will get to you and you will enjoy it. We received a report from your home which sounds very interesting and made us happy. Mrs. Cohn who is from this camp is now temporarily with you and she will give further news about you on her return. We anxiously await this. I am, today, sending you an envelope so that you will be able to write to us again and also a preaddressed, stamped postcard that you

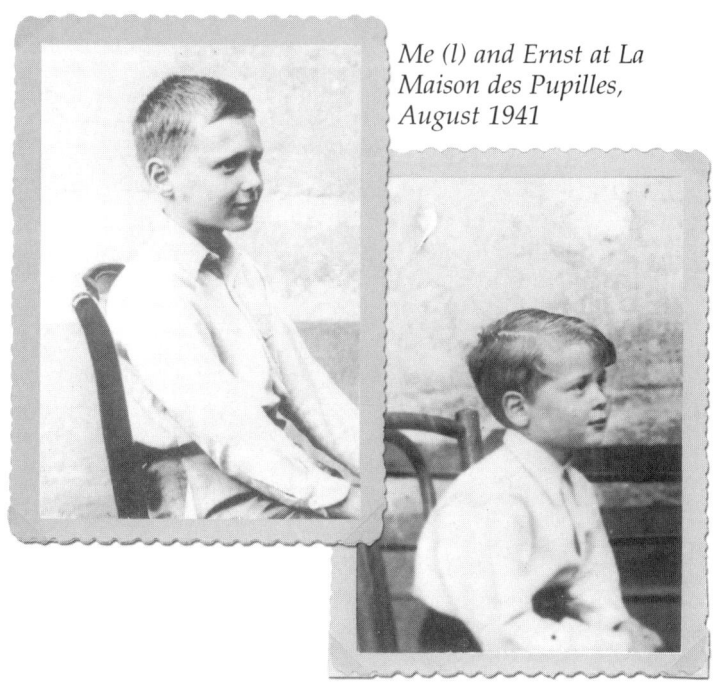

Me (l) and Ernst at La Maison des Pupilles, August 1941

Be Happy, Be Free, Dance!

can send to our relatives in Limoge. I could not give your regards to Leo's father since he was sent to Camp Récébédou. Many from here have already been sent away; we in Barrack 11 now number only 18 people. Uncle Ludwig and Aunt Tilde and Mr. Stiefel went to Récébédou as well. So my dear children, stay well, God protect you, let's hear from you again soon and be heartily greeted and kissed, your loving, Papi

My dear Richardle and Ernstele,

We heard that you are well and that your surroundings are nice. Play outdoors often, as it is healthy and gives you a good appetite. Did you have your pictures taken? We would enjoy one very much. Do you already speak French well? Let us know how you spend your day. Be greeted and kissed from your loving Mutti.

April 7, 1941

My Dear Children,

I and dear Mutti enjoyed your various letters very much. We wanted to write to you before but only had a chance today. I will give you news on a regular basis in the future. I was especially happy with your letter which included a report from Mrs. Cohn who informed me of your good health. I will now respond to your individual lines. <u>My beloved Ernstele</u> I am happy that you are healthy again and discharged from the infirmary. Continue to stay healthy and eat nicely so that you will gain weight. I was glad to hear that all the sweets tasted good. We received them from our relatives and as soon as we get more, we will send you another package. It is indeed good that you both are able to take lots of walks and enjoy your sports. You have good supervision and Mrs. Cohn will certainly look after you. We were elated with your precious letter which you dictated to her. Do so frequently and in detail so that we are informed of everything and above all, are aware of all that concerns you. I am glad that the black shirt fits you well and you can use it. Do you pray daily and how are you doing with the French language? Write a detailed letter soon again; stay well and happy. With hearty greetings and kisses from your ever-loving Papi.

La Maison des Pupilles

My Beloved Richardle, Mutti and I were joyous when we received your nice letter. Keep writing often as it always gives us great pleasure. We will send a package to you again with the lock you have requested as soon as I can obtain one. I will also include the writing paper. You write about money. Did you use up the 30 Francs which I gave you to take with you when you left here? Write to me more about that and if necessary, I will send you something. I am enclosing a pre-stamped envelope in this letter. It is very gratifying that the food tastes good; it will make you big and strong. I am pleased that you want me to send you additional laundry forms. That shows your sense of order, and it is good that your laundry is being numbered. Your letter for Mr. Wallenstein was returned here. Mr. Wallenstein was recently sent to camp Récébédou. Uncle Ludwig and Aunt Thilde were sent there as well and I forwarded your letter to them. That camp is located near Toulouse. Mr. Stiefel is no longer here but in Récébédou as well. I will send him your regards. I understand that you were happy to receive the parcel from Oma. It was so nice of her and perhaps she can send another. It was very thoughtful of you to inquire about Mutti. Thank God she feels better but she is still sick and in the infirmary. But hopefully she will soon be able to get out of bed. Dear Richardle, you write that you have a nice balcony and a big yard and also a white dog. You must really have it good. I will now close and hope that this letter will again bring you joy. Dear Mutti will add some lines. Stay well my dear child, learn well, take care of Ernstele, write soon again in detail and be heartily greeted and kissed from your loving Papi.

My Dear Richardle and my Dear Ernstele!

We always enjoy receiving a letter from you. It seems that you like it very much there and you are allowed to play, to go on hikes often, have nice beds and are together. Dear Richardle watch out carefully for Ernstele. Are you allowed to take the white dog on hikes with you? Passover is coming soon; will you get Matzohs? You certainly hear from Oma often. Opa is good and I also feel better. And so Ernstele dictate again and *write soon as we get enormous joy from your letters. It seems you have gained very nicely, what do you both weigh now? Be well, play and always remain cheerful.*

Loving regards from Mutti.

I did not know that *Mutti* had undergone surgery for breast cancer prior to our deportation from Ludwigshafen. The word "cancer" was taboo; no one spoke of it. Probably while she was in the hospital, Ernst and I were "vacationing" with *Oma's* relatives at their farmhouse in Rockenhausen – a place we loved – and I assume her cancer was in remission prior to deportation. I don't know if the recurrence was coincidental or a result of the stress and anxiety of our forced departure and depraved new life, but just two months after our arrival in Gurs, *Mutti* was bedridden for what we children thought was rheumatism. Shortly after we were taken to the orphanage, *Papi* notified us that *Mutti* was transferred to the infirmary barrack. Almost every letter from our parents contained a brief report on *Mutti's* condition. Most were optimistic but some mentioned her pain. The only doctors at Gurs were fellow inmates, who had neither medication nor painkillers; drugs would not be wasted on Jews. *Mutti's* health deteriorated steadily and her pain became unbearable. Still, letters and postcards from *Camp de Gurs* conveyed eternal optimism. They expressed concerns for our happiness and welfare, for our educational progress and development. There is no mention of the hardship and worries my parents and relatives endured. Of course, all mail was opened and censored. Sensitive information was blacked out with indelible ink, which we couldn't eliminate without destroying the correspondence. Letters and postcards that were too critical or descriptive never reached us. Some of those that we saved appear below and in the Appendix.

La Maison des Pupilles

April 17, 1941

My Dear Children!

I was very happy to receive your letter dear Richardle. Thank you for your report. It always pleases me that Ernstele is also well and I pray to God daily that He keeps you healthy. Hopefully it will not be too long until Mutti, you two and I will again be together and we can catch up on everything. Mutti always has much pain and still lies in the infirmary but I hope that she will soon get better. I feel good, meaning I'm well. So referring to your letter, my dear Richardle, I am always pleased when you ask how Mutti is doing because that indicates your concern. I am enclosing the two stamps you requested and will send you more next week. That is, I will send pre-addressed envelopes. I am pleased that you have good weather, you can therefore play outdoors. It is also warm here now. Thanks very much for the regards from Leo, Manfred and Hans, greet them likewise. Mr. Stahl, the teacher, is still here but he is sick and lies in the infirmary, so I could not yet give him your regards but will do so in the next days. In any case it is very nice of you to think about him. Teacher Durlacher is no longer here. A few days ago he was sent to Le Milles (another Camp). A letter from Oma arrived today. She is well and awaits mail from you. Buy some fruit, dates and nuts for yourselves occasionally and write to me at once if you have no more money and I will send you some. I delivered your regards to the people in Barrack 11 and they all thank you much and want me to send you greetings as well. The Elikanns are no longer with us, they were sent to Récébédou. Dear Richardle, you asked if I still had my position. Yes I still have it and much more. I took over the leadership of the Religious services since Mr. Openheimer was sent away from here. I am also on the committee to obtain matzohs and other things for the îlot's Passover kitchen. I am no longer in charge of the children's food preparation since there aren't any children here anymore. Dear Richardle, it was very thoughtful of you to congratulate both of us for our birthdays. I had mine yesterday, and Mutti will have hers on 4/24. I thank you for remembering. I visited with Mutti and we spent some pleasant hours together. Hopefully we will all be well and together on our

Be Happy, Be Free, Dance!

next birthdays. Dear Mutti made up a very nice birthday poem for me and had arranged for something for me to eat. I sent you a package last Friday containing 12 pairs of socks, 1 pair shoes, 1 pair sandals, 1 paint box, 2 balls, 2 loden coats with hoods, 1 suit (jacket and pants), 1 stocking, 1 pair linen pants, 1 white shirt, 1 red shirt, 1 blue wrap-around apron, 1 children's handkerchief, writing paper, 2 chocolate bars, 1 large and 1 small nougat bar, and 2 matzos. I hope that this package is delivered to you in good order. I had to send it by rail and was not able to pay for it as the receiver must do so. Let me know what the cost was so that I can reimburse them. Unfortunately, I was not able to obtain a lock yet. This letter remained here over the holidays, so I will add some lines today, 4/20/41. I gave your regards to Teacher Stahl and he greets you in return. In the meantime, I received your dear letter of 4/8 addressed to Mutti for which I thank you much. It appears that delivery took longer than usual. It was nice that Mr. Stiefel wrote to you and it was proper for you to have answered. I had to laugh over your report of Ernstele playing with the streetcar on the school desk. He loved doing that at home also. Uncle Willy's address is: Dr. Willie Frank, 3 Rue des Petites Maisons, Limoges (Haute-Garonne). Now I think my dear children, I have written enough. I close with the wish that you will stay healthy and that all should be good with you. Write soon again and be lovingly greeted and kissed from your Papi

My Dear Richardle and my dear Ernstele,

We were very happy with your lines Richardle. I am still confined to bed but hope that I will be able to get up when the weather turns warmer. I will be glad if you, Ernstele, will dictate some lines to Richardle again. Continue to play nicely, go often in the fresh air, and give regards to Mrs. Cohen. Be heartily kissed from your loving Mutti

Camp de Gurs, April 21, 1941

My Dear Children!

A long letter written by Mutti and myself went out to you today. After it was mailed, I received your letter of April 18 addressed to Mutti. We were happy to know that you are well. I am really thankful that you, my dear Richardle, write with such enthusiasm and that Ernstele dictated something. Do so often. You inquired about Opa. He wrote that he is healthy and as soon as he can, he will go to America. Oma and all of us should soon follow, so that we will all be together again. Uncle Ludwig is in Récébédou. I am enclosing a pre-stamped envelope so you can write to him. Naturally Aunt Tilde is with him, but Uncle Muni is still here. So my dear children, stay healthy, and let us hear from you again soon. Please send my best regards to Mrs. Cohen. The nougat bar in the last package was from Uncle Muni. Since you wrote you needed money, I will send 30 Francs to you tomorrow.

Again, hearty greetings and kisses from your loving Papi

My Dear Children!

As always we were happy to receive your letter. Ernstele has dictated very nicely to you Richardle and we appreciate it if you could write every week. From Manfred's letter to his grandma, I gather that you had matzos on Passover. Were they tasty? We had matzos too. I feel somewhat better. Did you receive our package?

Hearty greetings, love Mutti.

You must already know a lot of French. Please write us a sample sentence to show what you have learned. Best wishes to Manfred, Heinz and Leo from me.

Here is a letter I sent to *Oma* and my parents at *Camp de Gurs*. *Oma* returned it to me a few years later.

Aspet, June 2, 1941
Good Shabbos my dear Oma and Parents!

How are you? We are well. It is very nice here. Ernstele likes it also. Sixty new children arrived yesterday and today. Ernstele can certainly use his sunhat as the sun here is hot. We

Be Happy, Be Free, Dance!

recently received a parcel from Limoges containing assorted cheeses. They tasted good to me and Ernstele. We just received your postcard. It is nice that you also received a package from Portugal. The chocolate was very good. I want to show you a picture from Ernstele's rabbit book. A boy drew it for me.

Hearty greetings and kisses, Richardle and Ernstele

We recently had passport pictures taken. Please send stamps the next time.

My Dear Boys!

We were glad to receive your wonderful letter dated June 25, 1941. You wrote so nicely, dear Richardle and dear Ernstele you dictated well. We can conclude that you are well which is of special interest to us. With the extreme heat, you must take great care not to go into the sun, certainly not without a head covering and don't drink too much, especially water. Always do the correct thing as your teachers tell you. You asked about Oma, dear Richardle. She is still here, and thank God, healthy and looking well. She wrote to you recently. What did you write about in your school essay and did you have to write it in German or French? Uncle Muni is feeling good, and he is still here in Barrack 15. Thank God, Mutti is feeling much better. She was transferred today, because the infirmary is being renovated. Mutti is now in Barrack 25, which was outfitted for the sick and near Barrack 20 where Oma is housed. Hopefully, Mutti will soon be able to get out of bed. My dear Ernstele, you really don't have to be afraid of the thunderstorms. We have many thunderstorms here too and are not afraid. The good Lord protects us all so that nothing happens. We are pleased that you have enough good food to eat. You must eat heartily so that you remain strong and grow. It is wonderful that the books please you and that you read them often. The one about the rabbits is so very nice. So my dear boys, stay well and ambitious so that you will grow up to be fine men. Let me hear from you again soon. Be heartily greeted and kissed from your loving Papi

I am enclosing some stamps for your collection. Our relatives in

La Maison des Pupilles

Limoges wrote yesterday that they will send a package of sweets and we hope you will enjoy them. Again hearty greetings and kisses, Your loving Papi

My Dear Boys!

As always I enjoy your lovely lines. I don't understand, dear Richardle, why you say that I write so little. Whenever Papi writes, I add some lines. I am delighted to note that you are healthy, that you have much to eat and that you are being schooled. Dear Richardle, you will soon know French better than I. Write to me some time in that language. And you dear Ernstele, are also learning well. What do you actually do in school? Do you play and paint also? Do you hike often? Do you live in nice surroundings? Are there woods and hills? Nothing new happens here. But now Mutti is located near me so that I can see and talk with her often. Thank God she is feeling better. Perhaps she will soon be able to get out of bed. We received news from Opa last week. He seems quite content. Did you receive the package of sweets from Limoges? Don't forget to thank them for it.

Stay well, my dear boys. I send you greetings and kisses. Love, Oma

Dear Richardle and Ernstele!

We were very happy that you wrote so nicely to us. Ernstele dictated well and he should do so often. Let us know if you received the package with the overcoat and if it fits. We are pleased that you are enjoying yourselves. Eat heartily so that you will grow tall and strong. Thank God, I feel better. Love, Mutti

Mutti died during the night of Thursday July 17, 1941 at the premature age of thirty-nine. Her death was incomprehensible to me. I could not recall having someone close to me, someone I so loved, die. *Papi* made sure that word of her death came to Ernst and me through

Be Happy, Be Free, Dance!

the orphanage's director and teachers rather than in a letter, and that we had the support and distraction of our friends. At that time it was possible to be buried in an individual grave at the cemetery outside the compounds. *Papi* estimated that over five hundred mourners attended *Mutti's* funeral and many eulogies were delivered. The camp administration issued a death certificate and fellow prisoners created a homemade one on which *Papi* filled in the personal information.

Papi had written a letter after *Mutti's* funeral which was copied and sent to all the relatives: The translation follows:

Camp de Gurs　　　　　　　　　　　　*August 7, 1941*

In memoriam of my dearly beloved Schatzele (treasure).

I write these lines with unspeakable sadness and a broken heart, in memory of my dear, good Schatzele, deceased much too early, my dear, good, unforgettable wife, Lilly Weilheimer nee Wetzler, born April 24, 1902 in Ludwigshafen on the Rhein.

My beautiful, cherished wife died during the night of Thursday to Friday, 17 to 18 of July 1941 at 12:20 AM. In life endowed with wonderful, God-given attributes, aristocratic mind, bravery and noblest character. She was an exemplary wife, well brought up and a good, obedient daughter to her dear parents and a loving mother, conscientious to the smallest detail for her two little children, who are only 9 and 5 years old. At the most beautiful, youthful age of scant 39 years, she was torn from me, after regretfully only 11 years — during which time we had a happy home and led the most beautiful family life. Many, many rays of sunshine emanated from her to our dear parents, to me, to our dear, poor little children, to all our relatives and many friends and acquaintances.

The burial took place on Sunday, July 20, 1941 - 25 Tamuz 5702 - at 10:00 AM in the Camp de Gurs cemetery, Department Basses Pyrénées, southern France. There we took leave of the dear, precious departed, who had had to endure seven difficult months of sickbed. She was committed to the cold earth - warm love and many bright memories remain. Never before had there been such a crowd of about 500 mourners who insisted on showing the departed the last honor and many others had to stay back. Everyone lamented the much too early separation, a sign of my jewel's popularity and affection even here. Mr. Bauer, Mr. Altmann and Mr. Israel officiated at the graveside. In the eulogy the latter two described this remarkable and rare woman. I had someone record the ceremonies in writing to inform all my dear ones who live far from this unhappy place of the difficult fate, especially our father, the siblings on both sides, as well as the poor, dear little boys.

I felt very sorry for Oma, who had to witness this misfortune. Nevertheless I considered it lucky and providential that she was here in these difficult times. She nursed and watched over her own with great dedication and visited as much as possible. Certainly her most rewarding thanks were the last words of the dear departed:"Mutter, Mutter." (Mother, Mother). I visited my greatest treasure daily during her seven month long sickbed confinement, and I had lingered with Oma at her bedside, just three hours before. Nobody, not even the doctor, believed that she would die so soon. Uncle Muni, who did so much for the patient in sick days as well as healthy days, and with whose attentions she was always delighted, also visited Lilly very often and took a brotherly interest in her misfortune. She reciprocated his love with much care. She absolutely wanted him to accompany us to the USA. He, too, lost a lot and I thank him in the name of my most beloved "Schatzele" and also very specially in my name, for all he did.

We were stricken by this calamity, the memories remain. My good "Schatzele" was committed to the cold ground. How differently had my dear one imagined it. During her migration to a new homeland, my faithful, most valuable gem, was torn from me much too early. I still wanted to take care of her and nurse her but God wanted it otherwise and called her to himself all too soon. Mr. Altmann said, among other things, that because she had already performed so many mitzvahs (good deeds), she had fulfilled her life at a young age. Mr. Israel, in his

Be Happy, Be Free, Dance!

Memorial to Mutti, by the inmates at Camp de Gurs, July, 1941

eulogy, used a part of a beautiful poem that she composed here. Mr. Grombacher, on behalf of the home community of Ludwigshafen on the Rhein, bid dear Lilly a heartfelt farewell which deeply affected all those present.

For us there remains the enormous grief – I am shattered, my life is ruined. But I don't want to be angry at God. And I want to continue to live in the spirit of my dear, good, deceased, for the sake of my dear little children, Richardle and Ernstele, who have to do without their mother's love much too early. Since February 24, 1941 they have been in the children's home at La Maison des Pupilles in Aspet, Haute Garonne, Southern France. I also want to mention our physician Dr. Neumann, who always was especially nice to dear Lilly. A few weeks ago, when he was relocated, he bid goodbye with the following words: "Stay as you are, you are a philosopher and a silent heroine." That is how she lived. No complaint ever crossed her lips; she always wanted to let the sun shine in and give joy.

And so I want to conclude this sad misfortune. I will never forget what she meant to me. I still can't comprehend that she is no longer among the living. I continue to feel united with her. I don't want to undertake anything that would not be in accordance with her wishes, and I want to inculcate that into my "kinderchen" (children) for their own good and blessing. I want to ask myself with everything I do: "how would my good 'Schatzele' have done it?" May God protect our dear kinderchen, help them over their great loss and may He let them soon find a new home and a new homeland with the loved ones in the USA. May they, in memory of their exceedingly good Mutti, grow up to be good, able and useful human beings.

And today, since I lost my most beloved "Schatzele" and had to part from her, I have the need to act as I did on the day of our civil wedding, April 3, 1930, with a thank you to the dear, good parents. At that time, I sent her parents flowers with a note stating: "I thank you, dear parents, for the precious gift entrusted to me. Be assured of Lilly's happiness and visit her often in her own home." My dear, good parents, today I want to render those thanks again. May you find consolation and may you go towards a happier future.

In great sadness and gratefulness, Your Max

The Yahrzeit (anniversary date) of the dear departed shall be holy for us – this writing is a memorial.

Be Happy, Be Free, Dance!

Mutti's graveside eulogy appears on page 178. The letter that follows was the first communication from *Papi* after *Mutti's* death with lines from *Oma* added:

Gurs, July 30, 1941
My Dear Good Children!

Dear, good and wonderful Mutti sadly died as the Director has notified you. Today, I received the word that you were informed. I thank the Director very much for that as well as Mrs. Zwilling, who we are informed also takes good care of you. Give hearty regards from me to both. The dear God and the holy spirit of dear Mutti who will always watch over us also thanks them. Heartfelt thanks for the wonderful letter from the Director and the children – your dear friends, and for your nice letter dear Richardle. All correspondence affected me deeply and the condolences and expressions of sympathy did me good. I can't thank each individual so please let them all read this letter. Thank God I have much work here.

Mutti's pains were always increasing, and as dear God meant well with her, after she had been bedridden for 7 months, he relieved her of her terrible suffering. You surely will remember our good, beautiful, wonderful Mutti and I have many pictures and notations in your photo albums, which we will look at often in the future together.

Our dear Mutti died during the night of Thursday July 18, 1941.

The burial was on Sunday the 20th of July. She was very esteemed, loved and honored; which was obvious, as there were approximately 500 mourners in attendance. The eulogy was delivered by Mr. Altmann, prayer leader of Block E, Mr. Israel, leader of Block F and Mr. Grombacher representing the home congregation of Ludwigshafen on the Rhein. I kept the speeches and the complete funeral procedures for you. Our dear Mutti was only 39 years old in April. To remember our dear good Mutti, we wrote everything down and sent it to the aunts in America for the time when you are older and understand everything. I will let you read everything then.

La Maison des Pupilles

Now we must stay strong, pull together and go on with life. Whatever we do, especially you, always consider if we are doing it in the spirit of our dear Mutti and how she would have done it, so we act correctly. Keep her in good memory and honor always as our golden Mutti has earned it. I have again registered you for a children's transport to our relatives in America and I hope that you will soon get there. Oma and Opa and I too will be there so that we will again be together. We will take our dear Mutti with us in memory and photos.

Your letter of July 23 arrived today, with the one you wrote on July 16. Oma is healthy and expects to get to Marseilles in two weeks so that she will be able to depart for America. I am glad that you are healthy, that all is well and that you are happy there. Also, that you are learning French and that Ernstele already knows so much. That the food is good and you both have enough pleases me very much. When you get a new photo, please send us one. My dear children, stay healthy, God bless you, write soon again. Be heartily embraced with best regards and kisses. Love, Papi

Keep this letter safe—Richardle, and watch over Ernstele.

My Dear Boys!

We waited with anticipation for the reply from your Director to make sure that you were informed that our dear Mutti had died. We must all accept what unfortunately cannot be changed and know that dear God has released her from her terrible pain. As your Oma, mother of your loving Mutti, I wish to tell you that she was to us, Opa and me, always a good and wonderful child who only brought joy. And you, my dear boys, especially you Richardle, since you are already so sensible and understanding, must keep the memory of your dear Mutti in the best of honor, and do the right thing. Be good, obedient and ambitious so that all of us, especially Papi, can be proud of you. When, God willing, we will all be together in America, we will surround you with love and guide you in all your endeavors. For the time being, you are taken good care of in the children's home.

Be Happy, Be Free, Dance!

Stay healthy my dear boys, write as often as you are allowed. Hearty greetings and kisses. Love, Oma

Letter Number 1
September 3, 1941
My Dear Beloved Boys!

Today I received your dear letter of August 27. It made me very happy and I thank you for it. I always feel good when I hear that you are healthy and everything is well. I am interested in everything you do. It must be very entertaining for you on the soccer field. I was always glad to play; it is exciting and fun. Tennis and basketball are also enjoyable. My dear Richardle, you wrote that you recently took a hike and saw a threshing machine. Do you both remember that you stayed in Wallenberg with dear Mutti last summer and I visited you on Sundays? There too was a thresher. Blackberries are good, but you must be careful that you don't pick any poisonous berries. As per your request, Richardle, I will number all my letters. I find this system very good as you will then be able to determine if you are receiving all of them. This also indicates an example of order. You drew very nicely, dear Richardle, a landscape with a beautiful tree, a pity that Mutti can no longer see your work; she too would have taken pleasure in it. But she will pray for us, especially for you my dear children. Do you both enjoy painting? Richardle, you want to know certain Hebrew names. I sent them to you recently. But I will write them again today.

Papi is named in Hebrew Mosche ben Simon

Opa   "   "   "   Chover Schlomer ben Mosche

Our Oma   "   "   "   Gidel bas Malke

Richardle "   "   "   Simon ben Mosche

Ernstele   "   "   "   Jakow ben Mosche

Our beloved Mutti "   "   "   Lea bas Gidel

If you want to know anything else, please write to me. I received a letter from America today. The aunts and uncles want us all to come soon. Another children's transport left for Marseilles

La Maison des Pupilles

Schreiben N° 1   den 3. September 1941.

Meine lieben herzigen Jungens!

Eueren lieben Brief N° 1 vom 27. August 1941 habe ich heute erhalten und mich sehr damit gefreut. Ich danke Euch, meine lieben Kinder, sehr dafür. Ich freue mich immer, wenn ich höre, dass Ihr gesund seid und dass es Euch gut geht. Mich interessiert alles von Euch. Auf dem Fussballplatz muss es ja sehr unterhaltend für Euch gewesen [sein], ich ging auch früher immer gerne dorthin. [...] Tennis und Korbballspiel [...]

Lieben Kinderchen, lebtew. Spielt Ihr gerne? Nun willst Du mein lieber Richard die Jüdischen Namen wissen. Ich habe sie Euch kürzlich schon einmal geschrieben. Ich schreibe sie aber Euch heute nochmals. Wozu braucht Ihr diese eigentlich. Also sie sind:

Papi heisst auf jüdisch   Mosche ben Simon
Opa   "   "   "   Chover Schlomes ben Mosche
Oma   "   "   "   Gidel bas Malke
Richardle "   "   "   Simon ben Mosche
Ernstele   "   "   "   Jakow ben Mosche

Unser liebes Muttile hiess auf jüdisch: Lea bas Gidel.

Wenn Du sonst noch etwas wissen willst dann schreibe mir bitte. Heute habe ich Brief von Amerika erhalten. Alle Tanten und Onkels schrieben wir sollen alle bald zu ihnen kommen. Heute ist wieder ein Kindertransport nach Marseille gefahren, die Kinder kommen nach Amerika. Kurt Berg ist auch dabei. Wegen Euch habe ich auch mit der Ose gesprochen, Ihr müsst halt noch etwas warten. Vielleicht komme ich bald mit Euch und Oma auch daran. Mir und Onkel Muni geht es gut das scheint wir sind gesund. Onkel Ludwig und Tante Hilde haben gestern auch geschrieben, sie sind gesund. Habt Ihr auch schon einmal an die liebe Oma nach Marseille geschrieben? Was treibt denn mein liebes Ernstele? Es soll mal wieder etwas diktieren. Nun, meine lieben Kinder, hoffe ich Euch genug geschrieben zu haben. Lasst bald auch wieder etwas von Euch hören. Ich schicke Euch anbei 1 Freicouvert u etwas Briefpapier. Lebt wohl, bleibt gesund, seid herzlichst gegrüsst und geküsst von Euerem Euchliebenden Papi

Schönen Dank für die Grüsse von Manfred Mayer, den ich bestens arrüsse.

Einlage:
1 Freicouvert
Briefumschläge

today, the first stop on the way to America. Kurt Berg is among them. I spoke to OSE but you must wait some more. Perhaps I will soon be able to go there with Oma and you. Uncle Muni and I are well. Uncle Ludwig and Aunt Tilde wrote yesterday that they are okay. Did you write to Oma at Marseilles yet? What is my dear Ernstele doing? He should once again dictate something. My dear children, I hope I wrote enough for today. Let's hear from you soon again. I am sending you a pre-stamped envelope and some writing paper. Stay well. Hearty greetings and kisses. Love, Papi

Many thanks for the greetings from Manfred Mayer.

The letters and postcards exchanged between *Camp de Gurs* and *La Maison des Pupilles* were dominated by the optimism that the adult world felt compelled to present to us on one side, and the innocence of children unable to grasp the reality of a threatening world. I wrote to *Papi* on April 23, 1942:

Mr. Max Weilheimer
Ilot A Barrack 13
Gurs
Basse Pyrénées
Dear Papi,
We still haven't answered all the questions you asked in your letter No. 27. We are very glad that you are feeling well and I can report likewise for us both. Karl Landau wrote to us that he already delivered the package. I was very glad that you were happy with it. We also received mail from Limoges with many beautiful stamps. I now have 215 in my stamp collection. I will write and thank them for this. Sadly we are not yet going to America. How is Uncle Muni? Ernstele's schoolwork improved somewhat. The weather could be better here; sometimes it rains and sometimes the sun shines. When you write to Aunt Johanna, give her regards and kisses from us. We are very happy that you are working with Mr. Eckstein. On Sunday, there was a nice celebration. There was a lovely poem written by a little

girl. I don't remember the second thing, but it hasn't been this lovely for a long time. The evening before last we were served soup, bread, potatoes and for dessert there was good marmalade. At the 5 o'clock bell, each afternoon, they serve butter or chocolate. It is always very good.

So for today, many regards and kisses, Ernstele and Richardle

Ernst and me at La Maison des Pupilles, Spring 1941

We were not aware of the Nazi's plans for our future, or more precisely for our non-future. Hitler's manic vision was to render Germany "*Judenfrei*" (free of Jews). This might have been possible, considering that Jews comprised less than one percent of the total population. But, as the German armies conquered country after country, Hitler "inherited" additional Jews, and emigration became impossible – no country would take them. Rescue was no longer feasible. Then Hitler expanded his *Judenfrei* policies to include the whole of Europe which he anticipated would soon be part of his "Thousand Year Reich." The *Einsatzgruppen*, (SS supervised para-military mobile killing squads) used carbon monoxide in sealed trucks and vans, augmented by machine gun squads, to murder thousands of men, women and children at a time, but this proved to be too slow and sometimes even too gruesome for the individual executioners. A quicker, more efficient method had to be found for the total annihilation of the Jewish "race."

On January 20, 1942 at a villa in the Berlin suburb of

Be Happy, Be Free, Dance!

Wannsee, a secret conference of Germany's leadership took place. Around the table sat fifteen German policy makers, eight of whom had doctorate degrees from universities. They represented the elite SS, The Gestapo, The Race and Resettlement Office, and The Department of Justice, among others. The unimaginable, heinous plan for the *"Endlosung der Judenfrage"* ("Final Solution to the Jewish Question") was laid out in great detail by the presiding officer, General Reinhard Heydrich. Much of the coordination and execution was left to Lt. Colonel Adolf Eichmann, the head of "Jewish Affairs." Since Hitler's vision had been articulated by his deputy, Herman Goring, as early as July 1941, little convincing was needed to obtain the commitment of this committee. The commander of the dreaded SS, Heinrich Himmler, had previously ordered the construction of *vernichtungslager* (death camps), in areas easily accessible by rail in Poland – an environment at best indifferent to Jews, and where the camps would not be obvious to the German people. Experiments using Zyclon B gas had already been conducted on small groups of prisoners in Auschwitz. This odorless gas could murder many people simultaneously and impersonally. The executioners who dropped the killer pellets from the roof of the gas chamber into the fake shower rooms did not have to see their victims.

The Western allies heard reports of mass murders but they deemed them "unconfirmed" and dismissed them as not credible or exaggerated. By the beginning of June, the BBC and statesmen in the free world had all been informed through smuggled eyewitness accounts, yet the Allies still took no action, raised no concerns. The Jews in Vichy France had no inkling of what was happening to their kinfolk in Eastern Europe, whose fate they were soon to share. *Papi*, like most inmates in Gurs, still expected liberation, and eventually family reunion. The first deportation to the east from Gurs did not take place until July 1942, but even then, no one knew where the people

La Maison des Pupilles

would be "re-settled." We, at *La Maison des Pupilles* knew even less and understood nothing. Though we did not lead a life of a normal childhood, we were nevertheless children.

Opa, still in Germany, had not gotten well, although he continued to send optimistic letters. The family got some comfort from knowing that a childhood friend of *Mutti* and her sister Nelly looked after him during his illness. Irma Brunnett was a devout Catholic who spent so much time in my grandparents' home before the war and learned so many of our traditions that she took it upon herself to bake *challah* on Fridays and deliver it to *Opa* at the hospital, no doubt at serious personal risk. *Opa* died on October 31, 1941 and Irma made arrangements to have him buried in the Jewish Cemetery in Mannheim. She maintained his grave during her lifetime and asked her son to perpetuate this care. *Mutti's* youngest sister, Alice, wrote a poem in *Opa's* memory. The last few lines translate:

The hope of a reunion is sadly taken away

Why does everything have to end so sadly?

No one can give us an answer

Only God is Judge over death and life.

Camp de Gurs, 1. Juli 1941.

Meine lieben Jungens! Heute erhielten wir Eueren lieben Brief vom 25. Juni 1941. Wir freuten uns mit Deinen lb. Zeilen, mein lieber Richardle, sehr und auch mit Deinen diktierten Zeilen, mein liebes Ernstele, haben wir uns sehr gefreut. Aus Eurem Briefe konnten wir entnehmen, dass Ihr gesund seid, was uns besonders angenehm berührt. Bei dieser grossen Hitze müsst Ihr Euch sehr in acht nehmen, nicht in die Sonne gehen, besonders nicht ohne Kopfbedeckung, und nicht zu viel trinken, besonders kein Wasser. Richtet Euch nach allem, wie Ihr es von Eueren Lehrern usw. gesagt bekommt. Du frägst nach lb. Oma, mein lieber Richard; Oma ist noch hier, sie ist G.s.L. gesund und sieht gut aus. Sie hat Euch doch schon einige male geschrieben. Was habt Ihr denn für einen Aufsatz in der Schule gemacht und müsst Ihr diesen in deutscher oder französischer Sprache schreiben? Onkel Muni geht es gut, er ist noch hier in der Baracke 15. Unsere liebe Mutti geht es, G.s.L. sei Dank viel besser; sie wurde heute verlegt, weil die Infirmerie neu eingerichtet wurde. Die liebe Mutti kam in die Baracke 25, die für Kranke gemacht wird. Die Baracke 25 liegt gegenüber von Baracke 26, in der die liebe Oma wohnt. Hoffentlich kann die liebe Mutti nun bald vom Bette aufstehen. Und Du, mein liebes Ernstele, lass schon dem lieben Richard diktieren; so müsst Ihr es öfters machen weil was dies viel Spass macht. Mein liebes Ernstele, Du brauchst doch keine Angst vor dem Gewitter zu haben. Wir haben hier doch auch viel Gewitter und haben keine Angst. Der liebe G.H. beschützt uns alle, sodass nichts passiert. Dass Ihr gut und viel zu essen bekommt hören wir gerne. Ihr müsst auch fest essen damit Ihr kräftig bleibt und gross werdet. Dass die Bücher Euch gut gefallen und Ihr darinnen viel lest ist recht, das Buch von den Hasen ist aber auch sehr schön. Also meine lieben Buben bleibt weiter brav und fleissig damit Ihr brauchbare Menschen werdet, lebt wohl ; bleibt gesund, lasst bald wieder von Euch etwas hören und seid herzlichst gegrüsst und geküsst von Euerem Euchliebenden Papi

Für Euere Briefmarkensammlung schicke ich Euch anbei einige Briefmarken. Die lieben Verwandten in Limoges schrieben gestern, dass sie Euch ein Päckchen mit Konfekt schicken werden, lasst es Euch gut schmecken.

Nochmals herzliche Grüsse & Küsse
Euer Euchliebender
Papi

6. Path to Freedom

Hitler did not disguise his aim to cleanse Germany of its Jewish population but it had initially been perceived as rhetorical self-aggrandizement that would dissipate with the collapse of the Nazi party. By the time Jews finally emerged from their denial, there was no chance to survive economically, politically or with dignity in Germany. As a consequence of the 1935 Nuremberg racial laws they had lost their citizenship and all their rights. Now stateless and destitute, Jews could find no country willing to admit them.

In July of 1938, under pressure to intervene, President Roosevelt called for a conference of nations. Thirty-two countries sent delegates to Evian-Les-Bains, France, and private humanitarian organizations were represented by observers. The aim was to find places of refuge, even temporary sanctuaries that would admit the now stateless Jews. It was a hypocritical mockery. One delegate after another stated why their country would not or could not accept any Jews. Australia was proud they had no racial problems and did not want to import one. Canada claimed they already had too many Jews and didn't want more. Britain, which had a mandate over the ancient Jewish homeland of Palestine, kept Jewish immigration low to protect their interests in the Arab world and their access to oil. The United States cited the recent depression and unemployment. This great nation of immigrants, the land of the free, whose Statue of Liberty is a beacon of hope to the oppressed of the world, and which had absorbed hundreds of thousands of poor, persecuted refugees in the past, now in this time of critical need declared its shores off-limits. One small country, the Dominican Republic, was the sole positive voice. They volunteered to take in 100,000 refugees, but ensuing complications substantially reduced the number actually admitted.

Even before the conference convened, the Nazis dared countries to be sympathetic to Jews and generous enough to take them off Germany's hands. Rescue did not happen. Hitler was neither disappointed nor surprised. He challenged other nations: why couldn't they understand Germany's desire to get rid of Jews when they did not want them either? The gathering at Evian assured Hitler that no one would interfere on behalf of Jews. It was true. The world didn't give a damn. That knowledge made *Kristallnacht* possible.

Thus, even while it was still possible to flee from the Nazis, anti-immigration policies made it difficult. Humanitarian organizations in the United States and Europe issued appeals to save the remnants of Jewish life, especially the children. President Franklin D. Roosevelt studied the political barometer and chose an ambiguous response. He did not want criticism for absorbing unwelcome Jewish immigrants into the American fabric. To avoid a public opinion backlash or risk alienating the Jewish community (which idolized him), he deferred all decisions and responsibilities to the State Department which included many anti-Semites. Undersecretary Breckenridge Long, in charge of supervising immigration, deliberately imposed ever-changing requirements to hinder and forestall entry of Jews into the United States. Affidavits attesting to all kinds of political and moral information – supposedly to guarantee that the immigrant would pose no threat – became necessary. Compliance with these procedures caused tremendous delays, often long enough for other previously approved papers to expire. The State Department then mandated waiting periods before rejected applicants could reapply. Many members of Congress were also bigoted, reflecting the attitude of a large portion of American society at that time.

During the 1930's and 1940s, fears of anti-Semitism so immobilized American Jewish leadership that they generally became impotent. With few exceptions, they were unsuccessful in making a strong case on behalf of the refugees. In February 1939, Senator Robert Wagner of New York co-sponsored a bill which would have admitted 20,000 children, who would be supported by private funding. The bill did not specifically mention *Jewish* children but it was generally known that this was the intent. Congressional opposition, combined with President Roosevelt's silence, caused the bill to die in committee before reaching the floor of the Senate or the House. By 1941, the American government had been hindering the rescue of European Jews for several years while hiding behind misleading statements and false information. Only about ten percent of the existing quota was filled.

In May 1939, the steamer St. Louis left Hamburg, Germany bound for Cuba carrying 937 passengers – all but six of them Jewish refugees. Unbeknownst to them, even before the ship had departed, the Germans had rescinded their visas. Meanwhile, in an effort to promote further anti-Semitism, German sympathizers in Havana organized demonstrations against Jewish immigration. As the ship anchored, only thirty passengers were allowed to disembark. After days of futile negotiations, the captain appealed to the U.S. government to allow the threatened human cargo temporary entry. The steamer was within sight of America when the Coast Guard dispatched patrol boats from Fort Lauderdale to prevent it from docking and to keep the passengers from swimming to freedom. In desperation, the refugees sent a telegram to President Roosevelt, but their plea for asylum went unanswered. The St. Louis had to return to Europe, still loaded with rejected refugees. England agreed to accept 288; they ultimately survived the Holocaust. The rest were absorbed into France, the Netherlands and Belgium where they eventually fell once more into Nazi hands. Very few survived.*

Meanwhile, several organizations were working to save Jewish children in Vichy France. The most active and influential was *Oeuvre de Secours aux Enfants* (OSE). This group originated in St. Petersburg, Russia, in 1912 to protect the health and welfare of Jewish children. It relocated to Berlin after the Russian Revolution, and after Hitler rose to power, it moved to Paris. In June 1940, when Paris fell to the Nazis, OSE established "safe houses" in Marseille where they sheltered several hundred Jewish children. Given the obstacles and barriers that confronted them, it was logical that they agreed to partner with the American Friends Service Committee (the Quakers) which helped protect additional Jewish youngsters. Much of their work was done quietly, so as not to jeopardize additional lives. Many individual farmers and villagers in southern France were also kind, and they deserve credit for their compassion. As Vichy's hold on foreign Jews tightened, OSE and the American Friends Service Committee took on the awesome responsibility of choosing the children who would be taken out of harm's way.

Eventually, the US State Department authorized entry visas for 1,000 refugee children, but the Vichy government spitefully reduced that number to 500 when the American Secretary of State criticized French Prime Minister Pierre Laval for his ill-treatment of Jews. Then, when the Allies

---

* I should note that Jews were not the only victims of America's xenophobic and racial prejudices. Loyal Japanese-Americans, even native born citizens, were interned in camps for fear of fifth column activities. "Colored" people were restricted to separate beaches, toilets and water fountains even around the Nation's capital. But only Europe's Jews faced a life-threatening situation. The U.S. failed to save them, and it was a missed opportunity, especially for the children, the seeds of posterity.

landed in North Africa late in 1942, the Nazis seized the opportunity to occupy the rest of France, thus closing the door for any further emigration. In the end, only about 250 OSE children actually reached safety in the United States.

My brother Ernst and I were among those who were issued "Safe Conduct" passes (in lieu of visas), the equivalent of keys to the Promised Land. Alice Resch of the AFSC was in charge of choosing the children for the voyage. At my first reunion with Alice in 1998, I asked her: "What made you choose us?" Her answer was quite simple and logical. "You had already suffered the loss of one parent." However, I uncovered evidence at the AFSC's headquarters in Philadelphia, that *Papi* had relentlessly petitioned the Quakers and OSE to get us out of Europe. The fact that we had relatives in the United States willing to take us in and care for us, no doubt helped us get on the short list.

Letter Number 26   *Very Important*

March 30, 1942

My dear children!

I received your letter No. 24 of March 26 today, and I am rushing to reply to you at once. This time I was especially happy with your lines since I assume that you will soon sail for the USA. You will surely be happy about this, and well taken care of and attentively looked after. It is a relief for me to know that you will once again have your own home with our dear relatives. All the loved ones have written that they will gladly take you in, care for you, rear you, look after you and provide for your education and future. You will be welcomed and I therefore gave my approval for the trip. It is still undetermined when the journey will take place, although I would be happy if you could begin your trip soon.

May God bless you and look after you. I also give my fatherly

Be Happy, Be Free, Dance!

blessings for the trip and my wishes for a good crossing and a happy future. Give regards and kisses to all the relatives. My second request for a pass to visit you in Aspet has not yet been answered. I will follow up in writing again. If, however, a trip to you is not possible, I hope to speak to you during your trip through Oloran. We will surely be permitted to go to the train station. Other children from your home are expected to travel with you.

I am very sorry you did not receive my letter <u>No. 22</u> of March 5, 1942 but I really do not recall what I wrote to you. I have had many new work assignments, especially involving the Passover kitchen. Uncle Muni is well and happy with your news. He will write to you. In the meantime, he sends his hearty regards and wishes you`a happy journey. Uncle Ludwig and Aunt Tilde will write to you too. Your stamp collection must be growing. I am sending you a few stamps. Your hikes and games must be enjoyable. This is what we used to do in the past.

I am very happy that you my dear Ernstele are well and I thank you for your nice lines. You both have learned French poems which must give you satisfaction. The time passes and you are growing up. I am glad you were photographed and I anxiously await having a copy. You will soon get 15 days of vacation. Relax well and write to me. My dear Richardle, I note that you liked your outing very much. You certainly have nice surroundings. Your eating, as you write, is very good. So, my dear boys stay well and healthy. Happy Holidays and as soon as you know anything further, write to me. Hearty regards and kisses from your loving Papi.

Dear Director, Dear teacher Wildstrom and caregivers,:

I regret that I did not receive your letter. I am very joyous and hereby give my consent for my dear boys' upcoming journey to the USA. Hopefully they will have an uneventful trip without difficulties or danger. I thank all of you for your many efforts and the wonderful care my dear boys received during their stay in your beautiful home, where they have resided for over one year. I also wish to thank Mrs. Wildstrom.

Please keep me informed of the progress and accept my gratitude,
Max Weilheimer

The US State Department established criteria for selecting and reporting on children who would be allowed to immigrate to America, as is documented by the following cable from the AFSC headquarters to their office in Marseille:

Quakers   Nightletter
March 11, 1941

Marseille (France)

Cable Seventy-five State Department approves use UScom Blanket Visa for Hundred children and instructing Consul Marseille. Stop. You will identify children selected to Consul for quota visas. We anticipate no difficulty as quotas unblocked or open for all countries represented by children. If you foresee difficulty advise. Stop. In selecting take children under sixteen at time of application for visa excluding those coming out with parents or with mental and health defects unacceptable to immigration officials. Stop. Recommend children represent all religions, nationalities available and include some from Jewish Children's Committee Brussels now Care Secours Swiss Toulouse also OSE Unitarians and if possible one or two from concentration camps. Give equal consideration to those with or without relatives here do not include children for whom independent emigration possible, cable if these instructions not clear or you desire amplification. Stop. As selections made mail complete social medical histories each child with specific recommendations for placement where parents guardians so specify. Stop. Cable name, sex, age, nationality, religion, also name, address

Be Happy, Be Free, Dance!

interested person here if any. Stop. Unlikely children able sail Lisbon as one group asking Schauffler Press boat transportation facilitate Portuguese visas without specific ship reservations. Stop. Inform your overall costs listing details where you wish payment. We are trying to arrange affidavits for few children over sixteen outside above plan and will advise, need your estimate when first group ready for boat reservations.

Chge. American Friends Service Committee, 20 S. 12 Street, Philadelphia AFSERCO - (Relief)

Prior to our emigration, the Quakers needed background information. The documents, written in English, are now part of the archives of the American Friends Service Committee in Philadelphia. I did not know of their existence until the year 2000. There is a reference to a move the family made to Mannheim before my brother's birth in 1935, although every document in my possession as well as Ernst's birth announcement list our address as Bismarkstrasse 15, in Ludwigshafen. I was born at the "Private Clinic of the City Hospital in Ludwigshafen" but no Jew was admitted there after the Nuremberg laws of 1935, so I assume that the "move" was made to gain access to a medical facility which still would admit *Mutti*. The family profile below was gleaned from Quakers documents:

WEILHEIMER, RICHARD

Age: 10   Sex: Male
Nationality: German   Religion: Non-Orthodox Jewish
Birthdate: November 21, 1931   Birthplace: Ludwigshafen, Germany

WEILHEIMER, ERNST

Age: 6   Sex: Male
Nationality: German   Religion: Non-Orthodox Jewish

Path to Freedom

Birthdate: December 11, 1935   Birthplace: Mannheim, Germany

THE FAMILY

Father: Maximilian Weilheimer, born in Germany, 1887

Mother: Lilly Weilheimer nee Wetzler, born in Germany, 1902, died in France 1941

Both parents came from good upper middle-class families; the grandparents on both sides were teachers, and the mother was a well-trained kindergarten teacher, who, until the time of her marriage, conducted a kindergarten of her own with great success. She was the daughter of the President of the Jewish Community of Ludwigshafen, a woman who was greatly respected and admired. The father was in business and after his marriage fulfilled the functions of Secretary of the Jewish Community; the Weilheimers were loved and respected by their neighbors, and life seemed to open before them pleasantly, without cloud. The two parents were very congenial and the children saw only the happiest family life at home.

A good deal of special attention was given to the children's education. Richard was sent to kindergarten when he was three years old; he was of a sensitive and rather timid nature and did not want to be separated from his mother, but he quickly adjusted and the kindergarten teacher was full of praise for him. He soon showed great interest in handicraft and was quite clever at it. He still likes painting and drawing very much. When he was six, he was sent to elementary school and had for his teacher his uncle who had just graduated from the Seminar of Wurzburg, and had been appointed teacher in the Jewish school in Ludwigshafen. Even at that time the Jewish children in Germany had to be educated separately. Richard has always been a very satisfactory student, applying himself well to his work. On November 10th, 1938, most of the Jewish men were arrested and taken to a concentration camp and Jewish instruction was forbidden. For about one year, Richard received private instruction from his grandfather until the Jewish school was authorized to reopen. The little brother, Ernst, went to kindergarten in Germany also where he showed great interest and facility in handicrafts. The family moved from Ludwigshafen to Mannheim before Ernst's birth in December 1935. Meanwhile political events had been reducing the situation of this family; the racial laws had made it very difficult for the father to earn a living for his wife and children; the grandparents on the paternal side both died, and the grandfather on the maternal side (not legible).

Then in October 1940 came the forced transport of the Jews from that area of Germany into France, where they were all immediately interned in *Camp de Gurs*. Mrs. Weilheimer was greatly beloved in the camp, as she was well endowed with moral courage, and tried

Be Happy, Be Free, Dance!

to comfort and sustain those other unfortunates with her who were less able to cope with their situation. When she fell ill, the whole camp was affected and when, after several months she died on July 18, 1941, there was mourning amongst all the other internees. The children had both been liberated from the camp some months before the death of their mother. In February 1941, they had been placed with some other children from Gurs in *"La Maison des Pupilles de la Nation"* of the French State, at Aspet in the department of the Haute Garonne.

Mr. Weilheimer remains interned at *Camp de Gurs*. He is a very pleasant, obviously cultivated man, who shows great affection for his two boys, but he has been bowed by the misfortunes that have overtaken him. He considers that his own life is finished, and that he has nothing left to offer his sons. He is happy that they will be given an opportunity to grow up under normal circumstances in America, although the parting from them was very hard for him. The group of parents from Gurs had received permission to come to Marseille to see their children before departure. Unfortunately, they did not arrive until the day before the sailing; although they were not allowed at the pier to say good-bye, Mr. Weilheimer spent the whole day at the docks. The boat left at midday, but he stayed on until the day was over.

THE CHILDREN:

Richard and Ernst are a perfectly charming pair of brothers. Both have blond hair and blue eyes and seem quite well developed physically. Richard has a very sunshiny face which lights up when he smiles. His teachers report him to be very willing, cheerful and obedient, a child who adapts himself well, and is no trouble. He watches over his little brother with real affection, does very satisfactory school work, loves sports, is good-tempered and gets along nicely with the other children. He shows very plainly the fact that he comes from a good family, and has been given good training and upbringing. (When he arrived in Marseille preparatory to emigration, it was found that he was suffering from a rather bad case of Impetigo on his face and even in the hair. This received immediate treatment and cleared up satisfactorily in time for him to be approved for departure by the physician. It is very noticeable on his photograph, but its traces should have disappeared by the time he reaches America.)

Ernst at six years is a particularly appealing looking youngster. He still has rather a babyish look, with plump cheeks and tummy, and big rather coquettish eyes, and dimples. He is used to a good deal of affection and was quite a pet of the staff at Aspet. They report that he is intelligent and wide-awake, and that while he is not always obedient, his conduct on the whole gives them no trouble. The father says that the two boys have always gotten along well together, but that Ernst, the younger one, is the leader, and that Richard is the "Denker" - (Thinker) - the more thoughtful one. He hopes very much that the brothers will not have to be separated. Both boys speak some French, but have much greater facility in German.

RELATIVES IN AMERICA

Uncle: Maurice Strassburger, Apt. 33, 312 Haven Ave. New York City

Grandmother: Same address

(The names of other relatives were most likely omitted because they did not yet have steady employment.)

One complication made it highly improbable that I could be cleared by health officials for emigration. Due to malnutrition I had sores on my feet and elsewhere which refused to heal and I also suffered from a bad case of impetigo on my face and under my hair. I was taken to Marseille with Ernst and four other boys but placed in isolation for one week. It was very scary sleeping alone, in a tiny cubbyhole of a room. A huge guard dog roamed freely in the hallways supposedly to protect the guests. Strange snarling dogs had always frightened me so it was quite natural that I would never venture to the communal toilet during the night, but would instead pee out the window. Being uncertain about my future and separated from Ernst for the first time was very frightening. Fortunately, by sailing time, my affliction was sufficiently healed and the doctor was able to disguise the residual symptoms with a skin-toned powder.

Some events defy explanation. It was possible to obtain a short-term safe conduct pass out of Gurs but I have no idea what my father had to do to obtain one. Perhaps the authorities calculated that he was likely to return because many of his relatives were still in the camp. In any case,

Be Happy, Be Free, Dance!

I traveled to the US on this "Sauf-Conduit" in lieu of a passport

Papi met us in Marseille and we were able to spend one day together prior to our departure from France. In anticipation of his arrival, I had walked the streets with an empty tin can, picking up cigarette butts from sidewalks and gutters. I stripped them, collecting the tiny bits of unused tobacco in the can so that I could present this gift to *Papi*. He had long ago learned how to roll his own cigarettes. He in turn brought me some postage stamps for my growing collection. *Papi* also gave me a tiny address book containing names of relatives which he inscribed: *"My dearest Richardle to remember your departure - June 22, 1942."* It is the only memento I have of this final farewell. We could not possibly have imagined that this would be the last time we would see each other. Ernst and I boarded the French steamer, *Imerethie II*, in Marseilles but we did not sail until June 25. *Papi* came to the pier to see us off as he had promised, but I could not see him and he could not spot us in the crowd hogging the ship's railing. Armed guards kept everyone so far back that he blended into a sea of people. There were to be no embraces, no more good-byes, no kisses, only tears known to me and an unresponding God. I received the following letter from *Papi* after landing in America:

Friday, June 26, 1942

My Cherished Children!

I hope this finds you well, as is the case with me. Although I was allowed to spend a nice day with you on Wednesday, it was sadly much too short. You sailed out to sea yesterday, Thursday June 25 about 4 P.M. They would not allow us near the steamship. I would so much have loved to see you and speak with you once again. I went in the afternoon to the jetty on the harbor and saw the Imerethie II anchored there. But I could only come to the gate, some 200 meters away from the ship.

At 4 o'clock, I saw the gangplank retracted and anchor pulled, and shortly after, your ship was towed out by a small tugboat.

Be Happy, Be Free, Dance!

People stood at the pier waving and shouting their good-byes. Tragically I could not be with them and soon the boat was out of sight.

My thoughts were with you. So my dear, good children, I again wish you all the best and above all, good health. Travel with God. May He protect you and keep you well. May He provide you with a joyous future filled with good luck and may he allow you to grow into healthy, Jewish youngsters who can stand tall among men in this difficult world. You are so good, loved and upstanding and you will endear yourselves and be welcome.

I send regards from all the people here who know you, and they wish you everything good. I will be glad when you are among our loved ones and once again have your own good home. I hope to join you, that is what our dear Mutti wanted. We will never forget her. She would have loved to travel with us but God wanted it different.

I am sending these lines at once via airmail so that you will have greetings from me upon your arrival. I pray to God daily for you and your voyage which will hopefully be good. Take care of yourselves, especially in the heat, and you, my dear Richard, always look after dear Ernst. All will become right with God's help. You don't have to be so serious, my dear Richard. Stay happy, cheerful and good, as our dear Mutti was also.

I don't want to make a lot of words now, you already know everything. Travel with good luck. Oma and the other loved ones will await you and care for you. I hope soon to be with you again and to stay with you. Please give my best regards and kisses to all our family members and relatives. Now my beloved boys, stay well, and write to me often as it is my greatest joy and only wish to hear from you soon again. Regards and kisses, your loving Papi.

My address in Gurs remains as before. Good Shabbos!
And at the same time
A good Week
I will continue to collect stamps for you.

I believe we were on the very last ship out of occupied Europe. Five days after we sailed, the infamous Adolf Eichmann arrived in Paris demanding immediate implementation of the "Final Solution" for the Jews in France. Though individuals continued to escape from the Nazis and their Vichy puppets, mostly over the borders into Spain and Switzerland, it became almost impossible for organized groups, especially children, to escape. Beginning in mid-July the Jews in the concentration camps of Gurs, Récébédou, Rivesaltes, Des Milles, Vernet, and Noé – as well as the children in hiding – were rounded up for transport to Auschwitz and other death camps. During the next few months approximately 11,400 Jewish children and tens of thousands of adults were transported from France to the death factories. As reports of the true nature of these transports filtered back, the suffering and panic among France's Jewish population can only be imagined. Vichy willingly and actively assisted in the round-ups. Now there could be few illusions about the fate awaiting them in Poland. The free world had by this time been informed. There was no public outcry, and no action was taken. The victims after all, were Jews.

Most people say they had "no idea" what was happening in Europe, particularly in France at that time. But it is obvious that some knew more than others, and a few were trying to prevent a tragic situation from becoming even worse. For example, on August 10, 1942 Donald A. Lowrie, the European representative of the YMCA, wrote a lengthy memo to the General Secretary of the YMCA's World Committee, which begins:

In spite of attempted complete secrecy on the part of the police and as against a mass of rumors, here are the facts ascertainable up to August eighth. ... ten thousand foreign Jews are to be deported from non-occupied France within the month of August, their supposed destination being the Jewish reservation set up by the Germans in south-eastern Poland.

Be Happy, Be Free, Dance!

Lowrie's memo shows that he understood that the deportations were actually part of the Germans' deliberate plan to "purify" Europe of "undesirable elements" by sending them to death camps. He described persistent and ultimately futile efforts by the YMCA and the Quakers' to alert the American Embassy as well as the Vichy government and to try to stop the deportations.

In the meantime, we were at sea! For whatever reason, this French vessel, doubtless in danger of being attacked by the Allies, sailed aimlessly through the Mediterranean. We anchored off the coast at Tunis and then near Algiers but never disembarked at either port. Days later, we passed through the heavily fortified straits of Gibraltar and entered the harbor of Casablanca on the Atlantic coast of Morocco. There, all of us escapees from Europe were allowed to disembark and move about with limited restrictions. After a week we boarded the *Nyassa*, a Portuguese ocean liner, which carried about 800 refugees across the Atlantic Ocean. A total of thirty-five unaccompanied children sailed on the *Nyassa*, most of them Spanish. A few others from *La Maison des Pupilles* joined the six of us who had traveled to Marseille together. Someone had arranged for 'angels' to accompany us. An attorney named Alberti, his wife and two children, and a nurse named Paula Pfeifer were aboard the *Nyassa*. They did everything possible to help us. Our basic needs and concerns were always addressed. In appreciation, we wrote a "thank-you" letter to Mr. Alberti and Paula Pfeifer, signed by each of us. I still remember the illustration on the note: one child drew a dolphin skimming the ocean carrying children on its back. Mr. Alberti settled in Kew Gardens, NY, and several times during our first few years in the United States he would host a reunion for all of us from Aspet who lived in the New York area.

The crossing was uneventful except for a two day detour to Bermuda. That might have been glamorous in peacetime, but it was quite frightening in a confusing

U.S. CHILDREN COMMITTEE SS "NYASSA" JULY 10, 1942

COPY

No.	NAME	FIRST NAME	AGE	NATIONALITY
1	ABADIE VILARNEU	Elvira	12	Spanish
2		Luisa	11	"
3	BAUER	Lore	8	German
4	BODENHEIMER	Gunter	7	"
5	FERNANDEZ GARCIA	Corsion	12	Spanish
6	FERNANDEZ GERMINAL	Luis	11	"
7	FERNANDEZ GONZALEZ	Begigno	13	"
8		Manuel	11	"
9	FERNANDEZ OROBA	José	12	"
10	GARCIA ROMERA	Juan	10	"
11		Rosario	13	"
12	GIRON VALLES	Eusebio	7	"
13	HELMANN	Alfred	11	German
14	HERSKOVITS	Hilda	14	Tchech
15		Otto	11	"
16	HERZ	Eva	6	German
17	HESS	Rolf	7	"
18	LIEBERMANN	Herman	11	Polish
19		Joseph	15	"
20		Rachel	13	"
21	LLERANDI SISOURA	Maruja	9	Spanish
22	MAUER	Hjalmer	8	German
23	REICHENBERG	Dorrit	9	German
24	RIBARES SANMARTIN	Antonio	12	Spanish
25		José	11	"
26	RUIZ LOPEZ	Antonio	8	"
27		José	7	"
28		Juan	11	"
29	SAEZ CABANERO	Augustina	12	"
30	SCHILLER	Hugo	11	German
31	SCHNEIDER	Isaak	12	Stateless
32	STRANG	Esther	15	Polish
33	WALKER	Kurt	11	German
34	WEILHEIMER	Ernst	6	"
35		Richard	10	"

RECAPITULATION

11 CHILDREN (Half Passage)	5,500$00 each Escudos		60,500$00
24 ADULTS (Full ")	11,000$00 " "		264,000$00
35	TOTAL ESCUDOS		324,500$00
35 HEAD TAX US $8.- Each	DOLLARS		$280.-

The list of children who sailed on the S.S. Nyassa

world at war. We had seen French troops training in Morocco, warships at sea, and anti-aircraft units on the beaches of Bermuda. Somewhere between these islands and the shores of America we watched thousands of flying fish in front and to the sides of the ship. They formed perfect arcs as they leapt out of the water and dived back

Be Happy, Be Free, Dance!

REFUGEES AT CANTON—Refugees from Europe line the decks of the Portuguese steamer Nyassa, docked at Lower Canton today.

Ship Brings Over 800 Refugees From Europe

Portuguese Steamer Docks At Canton—Thirty-Nine Children And 150 Polish Technicians In Group—Oldest Passenger 99

More than 800 immigrants from Europe and the Near East, 39 of them children and 150 of them Polish technicians, arrived at Pier 11, Lower Canton, today aboard the Portuguese steamer Nyassa.

in several yards ahead. To these weary passengers they seemed happy, playful omens of freedom beyond the horizon.

The *Nyassa* was denied entry in the New York Harbor because of protective mines, so we docked in Baltimore, Maryland on July 29, 1942. Some of the immigrants felt confused and frightened when they saw many warships in the port. Agents from the Federal Bureau of Investigation, the Army and the Navy boarded the steamer and posted armed sentries to restore order. By the time we arrived in the United States, the AFSC had received the following thank you letter from *Papi*.

D.5 Camp de Gurs

July 5, 1942

Dear Madame:

Your very kind letter of June 26 with the enclosed card from my dear little Richard gave me an extraordinary pleasure. I am very grateful for this card which helped me to cope with so many difficult, anxious hours. I am also glad to hear that the children stayed with you before their departure for Casablanca, and that you were pleased with their conduct and behavior. I can confirm that my children enjoyed a good education during their earliest years, and that was principally due to my dear unforgettable wife, who was a model for them in every sense. The grandparents also contributed to their education, as they were both teachers. It is, as you write, Madame, so very sad that we no longer have the mother in our family. In the meantime, my dear father-in-law, a man held in great esteem who was known as a real philanthropist, also died, alone and suffering from a painful illness. My poor children have lost so much of the sunshine that they should have had, and we, the parents, have been denied the joy of raising them, and seeing them grow and develop.

My wife, who was a teacher, and who up to the time of our marriage had her own kindergarten, kept an album with many photographs for each of the boys. Fortunately I brought these albums with me, and gave them to my mother-in-law on her departure for the United States. I am very glad that I could do this, for they convey the background or heritage that I can give to my little boys, who during the brief years of their lives have already suffered such losses.

To my great regret I was only able to be with my children in Marseille for one day before the boat sailed; still I am thankful to the All-Powerful even for that. I was at the gates of the dock when the boat put out to sea, but my boys could not know that, nor see me. The pleasure of seeing them one last time was denied to me. My heart nearly broke then.

But now I wish to thank you for what you have done for my boys, in the name of my beloved wife, and in my own. I hope that the children will have a good voyage, and stay in good health; that they will have happiness, free from perils, and never in their lives have to submit to such agony. So much joy and beauty has been destroyed by the hands of man. The world which God created

Be Happy, Be Free, Dance!

could be so lovely and peaceful. We had a family life of rare happiness and contentment - unfortunately it was too short!

Again I thank you with all my heart. Please accept my most sincere greetings and expressions of profound esteem.

Max Weilheimer

7. A New Life

July 30, 1942 was totally confusing. Thirty five days after leaving France, we stepped off the *Nyassa* and into an unknown world. Thirty five bewildered children were delivered into the hands of strangers to begin a new life in a country and a culture known to us only by name. There were no familiar faces to greet us, no warm embraces, no one to reassure or comfort us. To me, America was a refuge, a place to wait out the terrible war years, a place to reunite with *Papi* and our relatives. I had never even heard of the "United States;" and "America" simply meant a land where I would be safe. Although we had supposedly gotten English lessons somewhere, I do not recall actually knowing a single word. I was a frightened ten and a half year old boy with one principle instruction: "Take care of Ernstele."

I don't remember how we got from Baltimore to Pleasantville in upper Westchester County, New York, where we found ourselves in a children's home or boarding school. We spent several days getting "cleaned up," with new clothes and some basic orientation on living in America. We also had to be reeducated in nutrition and hygiene. Our group consisted not only of the six boys chosen by OSE and Alice Resch, but others from *La Maison des Pupilles*, various "children's colonies" and "safe houses," who joined us in Casablanca. Individually, we felt bewildered, lonely, hurt, and abandoned – in a word: numb. Somehow we got through this first week on

Be Happy, Be Free, Dance!

American soil but it was difficult.

A bus transported us to New York City through the cavernous streets of a metropolis the likes of which we had never before seen. We stepped off the bus at the Jewish Foster Care office near 62nd Street on Manhattan's east side. Imagine the changes in our young lives: from an old industrial city in Germany, to a concentration camp steeped in mud and deprivation, to an orphanage at the base of a mountain range in southern France, to a vast city seemingly untouched by chaos. I had never experienced such a world of innocence and "normalcy."

I knew we were about to meet our relatives. It had been several years since I last saw them and I was apprehensive. What would my life be like? Where would I live? How would I be treated? And, when would *Papi* come to America and take Ernstele and me away with him? Ernst and I were taken into a room where two of my late mother's sisters, Nelly and Alice, waited to greet us. They had both married in Germany; Nelly to Kurt Stern, Alice to Maurice (Mor) Strassburger, and when their immigration numbers came up in 1937, they had the good fortune to secure visas and sponsorships for passage to America. I remembered them both and was happy to be with relatives for the first time in about a year and a half. Our aunts took us to their homes to live with them. Alice and Mor took Ernst since their daughter Eleanor was three and a half years younger and the prospect of treating them as "brother and sister" was appealing. Nelly's daughter, my cousin Margo, was nine months old and I was at an age when I could baby sit, so I was slated to be Margo's "big brother." Of course, this was to be only a temporary arrangement until we could be reunited with *Papi*. The Sterns and the Strassburgers lived a block apart on Post Avenue in the Inwood section of Washington Heights, which made it easy for me to see Ernst (whose name was promptly Americanized to *Ernest*) as often as I wanted.

When Aunt Nelly and Uncle Kurt came to America as

newlyweds, they were forced to leave everything they owned in Germany behind, as a condition to emigrate. Their small apartment was nevertheless warm and welcoming. There was only one bedroom so I slept on a convertible couch in the living room, and I had to fold my bed every morning upon rising. Baby Margo's crib was against the wall in the same room. Uncle Kurt was considered an "enemy alien" because he had not yet lived long enough in the United States to qualify for citizenship under the laws in effect during wartime. Since employment was concentrated around defense industries, in which "enemy aliens" could not be hired, there were very few opportunities for him. With little knowledge of English, he could not replicate his successful sales career in the old country, so he took a job as a shipping clerk. The European-Jewish Children's Aid organization maintained overall supervision of us, sending a representative to check on our well-being periodically, and requiring us to see their doctors for semi-annual physical examinations.

Oma, my beloved maternal grandmother was the only member of my family (besides Ernest and me) who was in Europe at the beginning of the war, who survived. She was the oldest member of our family who was deported to *Camp de Gurs* in 1940. Her brother, Dr. Frank who lived in Limoges, was successful in cutting through many obstacles and much red tape to obtain the prized documents that guaranteed her passage to the United States. He was the one who often sent packages of goodies to us at *La Maison des Pupilles.* While waiting to emigrate, *Oma* expressed her frustrations in a letter to my Aunts and Uncles in New York.

Marseille, August 26, 1941

My dear children!

Since your letter of July 22, I did not hear anything further from you. I miss your messages very much, especially because of my low morale which certainly needs improvement. Also, I did not hear from father, which of course contributes to my depression. I have been here for ten days already; I do not remember if I wrote to you that my new address is Hotel Bompard, 4 Therese Beaulieux.

More human beings are crammed in here than seems possible to accommodate, so I was only assigned a space last night. Most people who came with me and even those who arrived 14 days earlier from Gurs, sleep on the floor in the dining hall. Steffie was such a dear to take me to her room, even though she only has a single bed, so I did have a place to rest my head. A bed was vacated yesterday in the room which Cousin Martha shares with four others. Thanks to Cousin Toni's influence, I was promised that space. All the relatives are very helpful, which is especially welcome in our situation.

The emigration seems to progress sluggishly. Only one woman was able to receive an American visa since the new laws went into effect, and she is waiting now for a Portuguese or Spanish visa in order to leave by Sept. 1. How enviable! The affidavit provider personally went to Washington to plead her case, something which is highly recommended. Have you tried this yet? Today I tried to expedite my case. The man in charge asked me where my husband is. Upon my answer he looked concerned and said that I might have difficulties receiving an American visa. You can understand that I was very concerned. I immediately went to our relatives to consult with them.

Cousin Josef suggested that since father has already a reserved shipping number from Lisbon, but is unable to receive a visa from Germany, the best solution would be if he would travel to Portugal via Italy on a Transit-Visa through France. You should try to send the new papers from Washington to Portugal, where father could claim the visa. What is your opinion about this proposal? It sounds promising to me and I will write to Jak Benedikt in Switzerland, who will contact dear father.

Please let me know immediately, after you have thought about it, if the aforementioned way is possible and please write in detail to dear father. It is really terrible that obstacles keep getting in the way of becoming re-united with all of you. I am so pessimistic that I can hardly believe that happiness is still attainable.

A New Life

Hopefully, the fact that Aunt Johanna is still in Cologne has not become an issue. I suffered heavily from the great misfortune in Gurs and urgently await your direct news.

The separation from Max is very sad to me and he looks terrible. He endures the heavy fate unbelievably badly. Hopefully, the poor little children will soon be in your circle. I will have to go to the shipping company to change my reservation because departure on September 19 is not realistic.

Things are very active here, making corresponding and concentrating difficult. I met some acquaintances, who wait and hope. The food consists mainly of potato soup and requires many an addition. I purchase fruit, especially grapes. One needs money even here. Did you put in a claim about me not receiving the amount for May? How are you, all my loved ones? Hopefully, all of you are healthy and have steady jobs.

Hearty regards and kisses, your loving Mother and Oma

Oma arrived in America about eight months before Ernest and me when it was still possible to get out of Europe. She lived in Alice and Mor's apartment, where Ernest was soon to join them. *Oma* died in 1947, before reaching her 70th birthday. She had been in fairly good health and I have always suspected that her broken heart contributed to her demise. Being torn away from *Opa* so abruptly, and then so cruelly losing her daughter (my *mutti*) and so many family members, had surely been a heavy weight which she could never really overcome.

My first few weeks in America were not easy. Most of the people I had contact with were fellow refugees in Washington Heights, a neighborhood with the largest German-Jewish population in the United States. They had absolutely no comprehension of what I had experienced. Aunt Nelly and Uncle Kurt encouraged me to play in the streets with the "Americans" since that's where children who lived in apartments spent their time, especially during school vacations. The war was still going on and many of the kids had fathers or older brothers in the armed forces fighting the Germans. Since I spoke only German, I became a symbol of evil. They did not know the difference between me and the Nazis so I often found myself in fights. Early in my life I had been spit on and shoved around by the Hitler Youth for being a Jew, then there were fights in the first weeks at the orphanage because the French children didn't know the difference between us and the *"Boches"* who conquered their country. Then I was attacked aboard the *Nyassa* by anti-Semitic Spaniards and when I was set upon by misinformed Americans, I wondered if I was being punished for being born. Is this my fate? My life? Certainly, some altercations were not due to prejudicial intolerance. Some resulted from misunderstandings or my unfamiliarity with American customs, such as the time when a group of children surrounded me on my way home from worship at the synagogue, and swatted my new hand-me-down navy blue suit with silk stockings filled with flour. That is how I learned of a Halloween tradition.

The last letter anyone received from *Papi* was sent to my Aunt and Uncle. He began it in *Camp de Gurs* on September 22, 1942 and concluded it in great haste the following day.

<u>No. 5</u>

Camp de Gurs, Tuesday September 22, 1942

All My Very Dear,

Rosh Hashanah and Yom Kippur are past. When I think of earlier times, many memories come to mind. We became engaged on the first day of the New Year in 1929 and after so short a time, now I am all alone! <u>My dear blessed darling could not have imagined this.</u> *Thinking of Yom Kippur, of both parents' homes and our own, I remember that the whole Weilheimer family gathered in our home to break the fast and that my darling arranged everything. And how was it this year*

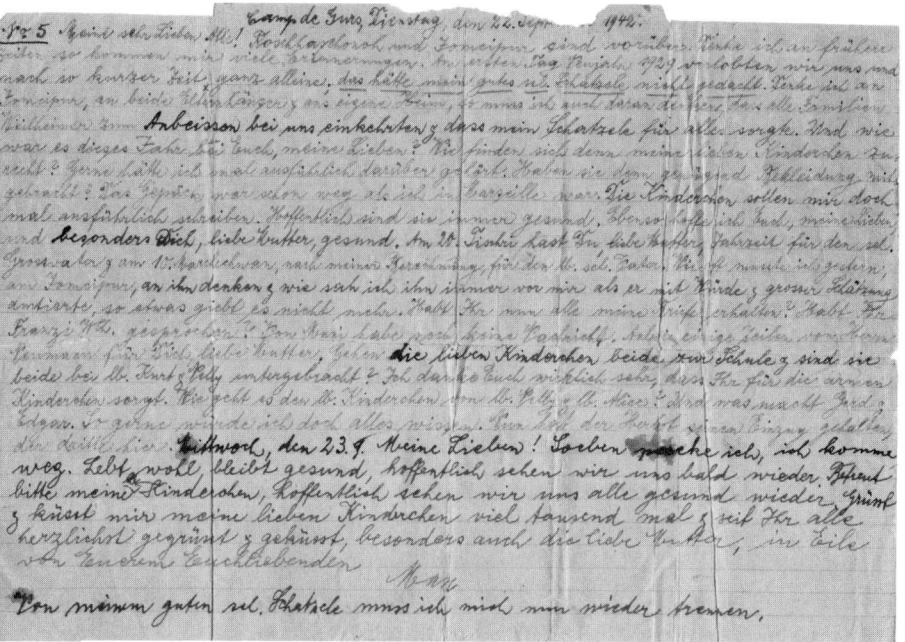

with you? I would be glad to hear about that in detail. How are my dear children managing? Did they bring enough clothing with them? The baggage was already gone when I arrived in Marseille. They should write to me at length. Hopefully they will always remain healthy. Equally, I hope you are all well my dear ones, especially dear mother.

On the 20th Tischri *you have the Yahrzeit* (anniversary of a death) *for blessed grandfather and according to my calculation on the 10*[th] *Marchechwan for blessed father. I thought of him often, yesterday on Yom Kippur, as he always acted with great dignity and esteem, which doesn't exist anymore. I have no news from Muni. Do the children go to school and are they both settled with Kurt and Nelly? I truly thank you for taking care of the poor children. How are Alice and Nelly's children? I would be pleased to know everything. Fall has arrived, the third one here.*

(The letter continued the following day.)

Wednesday the 23rd.

My Dear ones!

At this moment, I am packing. I'm being sent away. Live well, stay healthy; hopefully we will see each other again soon. Please take care of my children. Hopefully we will see each other again in good health. Greet and kiss my dear children many thousand times and all of you be heartily greeted and kissed, especially dear Mother. In haste from your loving, Max

From the grave of my dear blessed darling, I must now be separated.

We don't know where *Papi* was sent. It was not unusual to uproot prisoners on five minutes notice, giving them no information about their destination. Perhaps he was forced to join a labor detail. Many years later I located documents showing that he returned to Gurs and then on February 26, 1943 he was one of 975 men transported to the "collection point" at Drancy, near Paris. This was the staging area for Jewish prisoners in France who were deported to the extermination camps in Poland. Convoy number 50 was dispatched from Drancy on March 4, 1943 and it arrived in Sobibor two days later. *Papi's* name and that of his brother Ludwig appear on the roster of Jews in those cattle cars. Sobibor was one of three camps specifically built for the sole purpose of exterminating people as quickly as possible. Although the entrance gave illusions of normality, machine guns atop the guard towers were aimed at the electrified barbed wire fences. The surrounding mine fields contributed to its reputation as the most lethal place on earth. Upon arrival, prisoners' heads were shaved (the Nazis used human hair to insulate soldiers' boots and as filling for their bedding). Then they were herded to "showers" which were quickly sealed before huge Mercedes engines pumped deadly carbon monoxide into them. An hour after entering the camp

A New Life

With my cousin Margo, Aunt Nelly and Uncle Kurt Stern in 1955

almost every prisoner was dead. They never had a chance!

My summer had ended before *Papi's* letter was written. About three months shy of my 11th birthday I started school at P.S. 152 on Nagle Avenue. Since my education in Germany had been so brief and my understanding of English was limited to a few new street words, I was assigned to the first grade, a class of six year olds. I was promoted every few months to help me catch up to my age group. Not only did I miss a lot of work by never completing a grade, but the time I actually spent in each classroom was not as fruitful as it should have been due to my limited English, and I had little chance to form friendships as I kept leaving my classmates behind. My elementary school education had a lot of loopholes, leaving a vacuum that would remain for many years. There were no special programs for non-English speaking students but most teachers were very helpful. One had me stand up in front of the class (which was embarrassing at the time) holding a mirror in front of my lips so I could see what my tongue was doing. I can remember observing my teeth cautiously touching my tongue as I gently blew air through them, thus correctly pronouncing "the." The hardest sound for me to master was the "R." I was used to rolling it in the back of my throat as is done in German. To de-emphasize my accent, I would avoid using "R"s whenever possible, even calling myself "Dick," the popular nickname for Richard. My fellow students also helped me along, often unwittingly. In the fall of 1942 a group surrounded me and asked if I was a Yankee. I knew that "Yankee" was another name for "American," so I confidently and proudly said, "Yes," not realizing that it was the end of a baseball season and the favorite home team was the New York Yankees. I have been a Yankee fan ever since.

I tried to learn English as quickly as possible not only to make friends, but to show that I was a true American patriot. English was the tool with which I would build a new life. It was the unifying force, the thread to bind me to this colorful patchwork of our multi-heritage population. I went through the entire public school system, attending Junior High School 52 on Academy Street and graduating from George Washington High School on Audubon Avenue in June of 1950. Ernest's early schooling paralleled mine. He too attended public school 152 and Junior High School 52 before graduating from George Washington High in 1954.

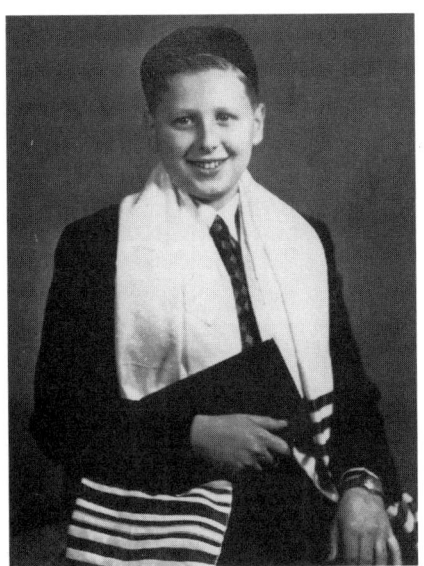

Bar Mitzvah photo, December 1944

My life during those eight years was fairly "normal." I started to refer to Aunt Nelly and Uncle Kurt as "my folks" since it was simpler than explaining why I didn't have parents. Unfortunately,

A New Life

we never talked about my former life, my parents or anything having to do with Germany, because the subject was too painful for all of us. I followed the events of the war very closely, taking delight at every Allied advance. With the invasion of France at Normandy on June 6, 1944 (D-Day), I became addicted to every radio news bulletin. I would check the map of Europe in the *New York Daily News* and note the Allied flags moving forward along the battle lines. Soon all of France was liberated.

My folks belonged to our neighborhood German-Jewish synagogue, the orthodox *Ohav Sholom*, founded by refugees in 1940. It was a storefront congregation on Sherman Avenue, sharing a common wall with an A&P market. During services, it was not unusual to hear the clamor of empty bottles rattling in their cases as they were dispatched to the basement storage area located directly under the *bimah* (podium). Along with the rickety slotted wooden folding chairs, this noise certainly added another dimension to our worship service. I attended Hebrew school there and was *Bar Mitzvahed* on December 2, 1944. This rite of passage left me with very confusing emotions: happy to have reached the age of Jewish maturity and responsibility, sad that *Mutti* was no longer alive to witness it. A symbolic part of the ceremony is physically handing the Torah from father to son. This was not to be. *Papi* had promised that he would follow us to America, but I had not heard from him for over two years. In delivering my talk, I expressed my profound disappointment that he was not able to stand on the *bimah* with me. I made a recording of the blessings, my Torah reading and my speech so that *Papi* would eventually hear it. But it was not until after the war that I learned, through various search agencies, that a cattle car had taken him to his final destination 21 months earlier, and even then I could not accept the unbelievable reality that I would never see him and my uncles again. My Bar-Mitzvah recording was never played.

Be Happy, Be Free, Dance!

After the ceremony a few congregation members and friends came back to our apartment to celebrate with a *Kiddush, challah,* wine, herring, cheese, and of course, Aunt Nelly's special cakes. The family remained for a wonderful home cooked luncheon. I received an ample supply of the customary Bar-Mitzvah gifts: fountain pens, neckties and wallets. My favorite gift (and also the most expensive) was a ballpoint pen. This invention had just come on the market and was exceptional in a frugal wartime era when disposable products were not popular. Writing with it took a little patience as it was totally temperamental and choosy about what surface it would work on – certainly not on anything that might have been touched by greasy or sweaty fingers. I don't remember who gave me this pen, but it must have been someone of means since it cost fifteen (1944) dollars; more than a lot of people earned in a week.

For years, we were known by the humiliating designation of "refugees," a label that automatically seemed to indicate a secondary status, persons with limited rights, grudgingly allowed into the country by the goodness of those who preceded us. We were not important or taken seriously. What did we know anyhow? We were afraid of offering opinions, of making demands or "waves." We did not question. We accepted any work, at any wage or condition and refrained from anything that would draw attention to ourselves. Our neighbors and sadly, some earlier immigrants who had been "Americanized," often demeaned us by saying: "You've got that refugee mentality." Coming over before war's end and long before the terrible truth of Hitler's all-out war against the Jews of Europe became general knowledge, I carried in my mind a "Pandora's box," filled with questions I was afraid to ask: "How could my family have been so victimized?" The answers were not available until I matured and was able to comprehend the political situation. Only then could I finally deal with my experience.

A New Life

In those early years, we contributed to our "refugee" image by looking out of place in our donated hand-me-downs, and embarrassing our fellow countrymen who were "smart" enough to have gotten here a few years earlier. I remember awkwardly wearing those ill-fitting cast-offs from distant cousins or Mrs. Somebody's nephew. Some shirts already had their collars turned and socks had been darned on the popular wooden egg. There was always enough food since Aunt Nelly and Uncle Kurt were very generous although their modest income made frugality necessary. At any time, there was a single box of cereal (corn flakes), one type of cheese (Velveeta), and cookies (Social Tea Biscuits) which were replaced with more of the same only when they were completely consumed. We never bought a soda to drink while out of the house, but waited until we returned home to quench our thirst. Dinner at a restaurant was a special occasion. I was often dispatched to the local grocery store where the clerk had to use his wooden pole with a grip on the end to grasp a single can of vegetables from a high shelf. "Uncle" Emile, the husband of *Opa's* sister, Hanchen, sold salami and fresh eggs door-to-door in Washington Heights and had a standing Sunday morning appointment in our apartment. He brought news and gossip from the refugee community, and he always left some of his inventory with us.

The U.S. State Department assigned us the degrading status of "enemy alien." I was embarrassed each time I had to report to the post office to re-register. Hadn't the government noticed my patriotism? I collected newspapers, bundled them and carried them, along with aluminum cans that I had flattened, to the collection center at school for recycling. Growing vegetables helped the war effort as well. My urban "victory garden," a wooden box anchored to our living room windowsill produced a small amount of carrots. I even managed to save pennies to buy "saving stamps" which were sold at school. I was very proud each time I filled up the book with images of "Minute Men," and exchanged it for a war bond costing $18.75. How could I be an enemy alien?

Some refugees sprinted way ahead of course, rapidly succeeding in education, business or the professions, but for the majority, it took time. Many people in our dense German-Jewish neighborhood wanted to retain their cultural distinctiveness, while others were nostalgic about their lives in pre-war Germany, at least until they learned about the death camps and the annihilation of our families. Despite their accents, others tried to hide their German background in public. When one person conversed in the old language, it was not uncommon to hear another say: "Speak English, you're in America now!" Of course the younger refugees learned English more quickly and seldom spoke in their mother tongue, the language of our oppressors, those murderous Nazis.

Though I obviously could not, nor would I have wanted to forget that I had a previous life and family, I was happy and well adjusted. I was determined not to be looked upon as a victim but to go on with life, playing with the cards in my hand. I wanted to conduct myself in accord with my upbringing and my parents' expectations. I needed to believe they would approve. I spent part of each summer with distant cousins in Cincinnati or with my Uncle Alfred Weilheimer's family in Washington DC. Uncle "Fred" was the only member of my father's family to get out of Germany in time and survive the Third Reich. During several summers I was also fortunate to be able to spend two or three weeks at camps operated by the Jewish Federation. The last camp I attended, Sylvan Stix, was a work camp: bunks, outhouses and even the artificial lake (which took about ten years of digging) were built entirely by teen-aged campers over the years. In the mornings we were assigned to work, but in the afternoons we were free to do as we pleased or participate in team sports. I helped on construction projects, and my main responsibility was tending the chicken coop. I never knew that one could get attached to chickens but I could not bear to witness the killings of my charges. I didn't eat chicken that summer.

Hugo Schiller, a friend from Gurs and Aspet, also lived

A New Life

The Maccabi soccer team, 1946. I am the goalie, kneeling in the center; Hugo Schiller is second from left, his arm on my shoulder.

with an aunt and uncle in Washington Heights. Four years after we came to America we located each other and resumed our friendship. He introduced me to the Maccabi Athletic Club where he played soccer and I soon became their goalie. Over the years I moved from Juvenile and Junior squads to become the goal tender for the First Class team. But soccer was not yet part of the American sports scene and only European-Americans supported the teams. The Star of David was part of the Maccabi logo emblazoned on our uniforms. Many of the clubs had German names like Shwarben, Eintracht, Hota, Hanseaten, and Phealzer; they were anti-Semitic. Fights would often break out on the field. In 1948, I was a contender for the U.S. Olympic team but was eliminated in the final try-outs before the competition in London.

In 1951, long after we knew that *Papi* had not survived, Ernest was adopted by the Strassburgers, an act which I did not support. I felt bitter and alone. I considered this a betrayal of the memory of my father whose last request to me was to "stay together and take care of Ernstele." Because of my wish to preserve the Weilheimer name and heritage, I was able to convince Aunt Alice and Uncle Mor to let him keep our family name. The Sterns had wanted to adopt me as well, but I felt that would mean giving up my family and my memory. Nevertheless, I was always treated like a son and I treated the Sterns as a son would his parents.

My aunts and uncles who came to America worked hard to build lives and homes for their families. They arrived not knowing English, and had a difficult time obtaining suitable employment. Neither their degrees from German universities nor their careers in education and social welfare were recognized. *Mutti's* sister Emmy worked as a matron in the ladies room of a Times Square restaurant. Aunt Nelly held a job in a small local factory, bottling cosmetics. Uncle Mor was the luckiest. At the onset of the Hitler era the company he was employed by in Germany relocated to New York and they rehired him when he immigrated to the States. Years later, he became their comptroller. Uncle Kurt lost several jobs when companies he was employed by obtained defense contracts. He eventually became a Fuller Brush Man, selling his wares door-to-door in the German speaking, non-Jewish Yorkville section of New York. Most of his sales were made by a small down payment followed up by weekly increments of a dollar or two. As I got older, I was pressed into service to make collections and deliveries for him. I knew it had to be done but I hated it. I was very uncomfortable walking through the streets carrying broom handles and cleaning supplies, and climbing the steps of the five or six story walk-up buildings to ask people for their money. Many of his customers were anti-Semitic, and not knowing I was his nephew, they would express hurtful remarks. But it was a living, and refugees could not be anyone's burden. Later, during my high-school years, I worked for a neighborhood dental laboratory that did business throughout the city.

A New Life

Although I would sometimes polish new dentures, my principal job was making deliveries. My starting wage was thirty-five cents an hour but increases came quite frequently. By the time I was a senior in high school, I was up to sixty cents. Wow! Sixty cents per hour translated to a whole penny per minute. That meant if I was out on a delivery and missed the train – or could stall or stretch a minute here and there – I earned another penny. I was in the big time! I felt like I had made it in America!

The years following the war brought revelations about the depth of German crimes against the Jews, and unspeakable information that to this day cannot be understood. One cannot conceive of a human being ripping an infant from a mother's bosom and smashing its skull against a stone wall, or tossing children into a fiery pit to die. One cannot grasp the image of cattle cars delivering human cargo to death camps. The Holocaust could not have happened without the support and willing participation of millions of Germans and collaborators in occupied countries.

In 1978 the French lawyer and Nazi hunter, Serge Klarsfeld, published his *Memorial to the Jews Deported From France 1942-1944*, based on the original deportation lists found in the Gestapo's French archives. Because of my self-imposed taboo on Holocaust related subjects, I was not aware of Monsieur Klarsfeld's work until 1993, but that is how I eventually learned my father's transport number and destination. I think of *Papi* on the death train so coldly and generically designated as convoy number 50. My inability to know his last thoughts haunt me still. Did he realize his two sons were safe? Did he know that Hitler's threat "today Europe, tomorrow the world" would not materialize? ... that Hitler's reach would not cross the Atlantic Ocean? Did he know his sons would make new lives, marry and father his grandchildren in a free and peaceful society? If only I could be sure of his vision and faith as the heavy metal doors sealed the death chambers.

As more eye-witness accounts came from Survivors and liberators – as the grim news about the extent of the murderous rampage came to light – we scrambled to get information about the loved ones we left behind in Europe. Jewish and international agencies were set up to trace the missing, to search for Survivors. Some were located, most were not. The German language newspaper *"Aufbau"* (Reconstruction) published in New York by Jewish immigrants and read worldwide, was full of ads under the heading of: *Gesucht Wird"* (searching for). Almost all were unanswered. Some members of the Survivor-refugee community asked questions starting: "What if …? Why didn't …? How come …?" Some became emotionally constipated, never releasing their invisible hurt, scarred for life. Others became disillusioned by their prior adulation for God-like figures, political leaders who they now came to regard as false idols. Many, especially the younger ones, chose to enter their next chapter, to acknowledge their suffering and losses, yet go forward, to create and thrive.

Ludwigshafen, in ruins in the late 1940s

A New Life

Shamefully, tens-of-thousands of Nazi war criminals and human rights violators were never held accountable for their actions. Some killers, torturers, guards, collaborators and those who greased the gears of the genocidal enterprise were anonymously absorbed into the German population while others obtained passage to South American, the Middle East and countries around the globe. The Soviet Union and the United States vied for those whose scientific, aeronautic or military knowledge could contribute to their quest for cold-war supremacy. Everything, including genocide seemed excusable. Only a handful of criminals were brought before a tribunal at Nuremberg and lesser courts, and very few have been brought to justice since. Most of them claimed: "We were only following orders" or "There was nothing we could have done." There was obviously a moral void. One should not be vengeful, but I must confess I was happy to see a 1949 German publication about my birth city entitled *"Ludwigshafen in Trümmern,"* (Ludwigshafen in Ruins.) Though the city had been bombed throughout the war, the biggest attack took place during the night of September 5, 1943 when almost 80,000 bombs rained onto Ludwigshafen in only forty minutes, and what had previously escaped the wrath of allied determination was obliterated. The city council determined that 124 air raids destroyed 86% of Ludwigshafen by the end of the war.

Like many in the Jewish community, I hated everything German with a passion. I would have nothing to do with the people nor would I purchase any products manufactured there. Even today I would not buy or even feel comfortable sitting in a German car. Nor can I tolerate their guttural speech. I have gotten off elevators in my office building when German employees got on. At times ambiguity tormented me. Eugen, the husband of *Mutti's* good friend, Irma Brunnett (who was also friendly with Aunt Nelly) came to the states on business. He had returned to his prewar banking career in

Be Happy, Be Free, Dance!

Germany after spending eight years as a prisoner of war in Russia. Aunt Nelly and Uncle Kurt invited him to stay with us for a few days during his visit to New York. Giving up my sleeper couch for two nights was not the problem, but I kept thinking that even though Irma had done some very courageous things during those terrible times, Eugen served in an elite Nazi army unit, having joined the party, ostensibly to keep his job. Every time I looked at him I would visualize him in a Nazi uniform, the offensive lapels, belt buckle and insignias, intimidating and threatening.

8. After High School and Into Another War

I graduated from high school in 1950 with low expectations for my future. Although I was raised by educated relatives in a community of downtrodden refugees, they discouraged me from following in their professional footsteps. The German Jews who fled their Nazi homeland did not feel entirely welcome in America and they cautioned: "it could happen here." They had a tough time in their new land, not knowing the language and not being able to get back into the professions or occupations for which they were trained and from which they were so abruptly ejected. They said "Forget college; learn to use your hands. Learn a transferable skill; become a watchmaker or something like that." They meant well, but I had no interest in sitting on a stool all day, squinting in order to grip a loupe while manipulating a pair of tweezers to align the gears of a timepiece.

Ever since I spent a part of my summer vacations in Washington DC with my Uncle Alfred, helping him in his small general store, I had enjoyed doing window displays. Though he mostly sold groceries, a good portion of his merchandise was seasonal and non-food items. How I loved using my creative skills to display fireworks for the Fourth of July! Getting into a store window, setting up merchandise in a pleasing, attractive and artistic manner was fun and I had a natural flair for it. I decided that upon graduating from high school, I would apply to a fashionable Fifth Avenue specialty shop and apprentice in their display department. But first came the summer, my last fling with no obligations, no responsibilities. Through a connection I was able to secure a job as a bus boy in the dining hall of Camp *Achvah*, a Jewish children's summer camp located in Port Jervis, NY. They offered me no pay, only the opportunity to share in the tips waiters received from parents on visiting days, and to be out of the city's sweltering humidity and heat. During our orientation, the director decided that the three female counselors assigned to the Kindergarten bunk of 4 to 6 year olds should be reinforced with a male role model. I got the job and was endearingly dubbed "Daddy Dick."

But my life would soon change abruptly again. On June 25, 1950, Korea, "The Land of the Morning Calm" erupted in armed conflict when the northern armies invaded the South. Japan had defeated Russia in the war of 1904, and become the "protector" of Korea. By 1910 Korea was incorporated into the Japanese Empire and its government was reorganized along the lines of a Japanese province. For the next forty years, Korea considered itself an occupied country. After the defeat of Japan in the Second World War, the "Big Four" allies (the United States, Great Britain, the Soviet Union and China) agreed that Korea should become free and independent. The Soviet Union had entered the fight in the Pacific during the waning hours of the war, so they were permitted to accept the surrender of Japanese troops above the 38th parallel in Korea while the American forces did likewise below that line. Both former allies soon withdrew their forces leaving two Koreas to govern themselves.

Both the "People's Democratic Republic" (the North), and the southern part of the country known as the "Republic of Korea," had resources that the other needed so they each claimed sovereignty over the whole peninsula. In a bold move on that fateful day in June, the army of the North, still a client of the USSR, crossed the demarcation line, claiming South Korea in defiance of The United Nations. The United States and its allies feared a "domino effect" – the systematic takeover of additional countries by the communist block. The sight of South Korea being swallowed behind the Iron Curtain was unacceptable to the United States and the United Nations. Within two days, President Harry S. Truman committed American troops to combat, in an effort to thwart this attempted takeover.

Our carefree summer was rudely interrupted as several of my fellow counselors in the armed forces reserves had to report immediately for active duty. Although I was not yet nineteen, I had been required to register with the selective service system, but I did not hear from my local draft board. The Korean War picked up momentum in the late fall as American troops, with some support from several United Nations member states, drove the communist army back over the 38th parallel. Then, just before Christmas 1950, the Chinese army came to the aid of their North Korean comrades. American troops retreated to a significantly smaller area of South Korea, and many young men were called into military service.

The draft board had not yet reached my number but prospective employers were reluctant to hire young men of draft age, especially if on-the-job training was necessary. The closest I came to obtaining employment in a creative field was in the advertising department of the R.D. Werner Company, at the time a leading manufacturer of aluminum for trendy Formica kitchens and bathrooms. (This company would later gain major recognition as a manufacturer of lightweight metal ladders.) I was hired by the founder's brother, a retired army colonel who understood my predicament. In the meantime, I pursued Liberal Arts courses at the City College of New York and studied window display techniques at the Pan American Art School. As a non-matriculated, part-time student I was not exempt from the military, so the anticipation of receiving the "Order to report for armed forces physical examination" followed by the "Order to report for induction" always hung over me. On November 20, 1951, one day before my twentieth birthday, I was finally scheduled for my medical clearance. Then, having been found fit for service, I received the impersonal notice from "The President of the United States …Greetings …" and was ordered to report for induction at the Whitehall Street location in lower Manhattan at 7:00 A.M. on January 31, 1952.

I knew President Truman was right, but I was not anxious to see war again. I had not volunteered for the regular army, but as an immigrant grateful to his adopted country, I felt it was my patriotic duty to go when I was called, without seeking excuses. I was convinced that we had to prevent Communist expansion on the Asian continent. Hadn't we recently learned the lessons of isolation and appeasement?

From Whitehall Street, I was bussed to Camp Kilmer, New Jersey, where our group spent several days in indoctrination and medical processing before we received our assignments to basic training units. I shipped out to Fort Knox, Kentucky and took my training with Company D, 84th Tank Battalion of the 3rd Armored Division. After eight weeks of extensive light infantry training on weapons, tactics and armor, I was physically and mentally hardened, but I could never get away from prejudice and intolerance. On one of our first days off, I was standing on the upper deck of our barrack with a member of our squad from Louisiana. Observing a colored soldier walking alongside a white nurse, my fellow trainee turned to me and proudly exclaimed "Where I come from, they'd string this Nigger up by his balls." I quickly took exception to his remark and explained that I was Jewish, anticipating his statement would be followed by an anti-Semitic comment. Somehow these usually came as a matched pair in an insensitive tirade. Startled, he said to me "but you don't look Jewish." "What is a Jew supposed to look like?" I retorted. "I don't know; but you don't look like one." He confessed that he had never knowingly seen a Jew. It was an era in America when Jim Crow was pervasive and discrimination an acceptable practice, especially in the Southern part of the country.

After the normal training cycle, we were invited to select an advanced program: Officers Candidate School, paratrooper or heavy weapons. I was not eligible for the first as I was not yet a citizen. (At the time, an immigrant had to be 21 to attain citizenship unless his parents had become citizens, automatically including the minor. Being orphaned, I had to wait for my 21st birthday. Or if this conflict had been a declared war instead of a "police action" as it was officially designated, I would have been able to obtain my citizenship papers prior to entering the military.) The second option was not for me. I probably have done some dumb things in my life, but jumping out of airplanes with a rifle and full field pack while some unseen enemy soldier with his feet planted firmly on the ground used me for target practice, was not my idea of an acceptable risk. So I chose eight more weeks of training, mostly on mortars and other heavy weapons. Then I was asked to take an interpreter's examination in German, which of course, I passed quite easily. Several of my fellow German-born trainees had chosen to go to Europe, but my hatred of Germany was so deep that I had vowed never again to set foot on its soil. Instead I allowed fate to dictate my destiny and I headed for Korea. That's where the action was. I was worried about not being a citizen, in case I was captured. I contacted Jacob Javits, my Congressman (later a U.S. Senator) who assured me that I would be entitled to all rights under the Geneva Convention.

I soon found myself on a troop train making the long journey to Camp Stoneman in Pittsburg, California. Our stay there was very short and restricted to base. I had just enough time to go AWOL and take in a burlesque show off camp. (What could they do to me if my unauthorized absence was discovered? Ship me to Korea?) A group of

Be Happy, Be Free, Dance!

us bonded at the beer hall on our last night while trying to remember all we had been taught in basic training, hoping we would not need to apply any of it. Then, along with approximately five thousand men I sailed out under the Golden Gate Bridge amid a strange silence aboard the U.S.S. General W.A. Mann. The dense fog prematurely stole sight of the shore from us. I wondered if I would ever see America again.

Our first stop was Camp Drake near Tokyo, where our personal weapons were issued and we had several days to "zero them in." The M-1 would become our most trusted companion on the Korean Peninsula. We would eat, sleep, shower and spend every moment within arms' reach of it. We knew how to care for it, take it apart, clean and reassemble it, blindfolded if necessary. Having seen war, its destruction and suffering only a short time earlier I never believed I would actually be a participant in such a human tragedy. I kept thinking: "This cannot be. Wake up; it's all a mistake, a dream — a nightmare!"

On July 29, 1952 – the tenth anniversary of my arrival in the United States on the *Nyassa* – our landing craft sped towards Inchon, Korea. From there, we traveled north on an antiquated Korean railroad. Alongside the tracks, peasants were selling souvenirs crafted from the brass of spent American shell casings. Being very sensitive to racial slurs, I was shocked to hear a GI several rows ahead of me, remark: "I didn't know they had Jew peddlers in Korea." Many of us came from the New York area so there were many Jews on board. Although I was startled by this prejudicial remark, I was slow to react. Others jumped the bigot and flattened his face, without any interference or repercussions.

Within days, I found myself in the Combat Zone, assigned to back up United Nations troops from France, Australia, Ethiopia, Turkey and the Republic of Korea. But most of the time I was located at company headquarters, a mile or two behind the front, where my official responsibility was to assign replacements to our line companies, and to maintain personnel records and data. During some skirmishes, I was assigned to ride shotgun for supply convoys. When we reached the line of battle, I would help unload ammunition and remain with the men in the bunkers for several days before returning to Headquarters Company. I served with good men and made a habit of never ordering anyone to do something I myself would not or had not done. Though we were always aware of the dangers, we believed in our own immortality. We denied reality. During my entire Korean War experience, I never had to fire a weapon at enemy troops.

I served in the "Second Chemical Mortar Battalion." The name originated in a previous war when the unit was responsible for creating smokescreens for the infantry, by firing mortar shells containing white phosphorous. The Communist enemy took advantage of the "chemical" part of our name, and turned it into a major propaganda campaign, by spreading the false rumor that the United States was violating international treaties by engaging in chemical warfare. The Department of the Army wasted no time renaming our unit the "461st Infantry Battalion (Heavy Mortar)." We saw a tremendous amount of action, set a record for the most consecutive days in combat, and earned the most individual decorations for a unit of our size. Our battalion received the Presidential Unit Citation for:

"... outstanding performance of duty and extraordinary heroism in action against an armed enemy in the vicinity of Kumhwa, Korea. During the period 7 October to 22 October 1952, when the Communist forces massed their strength and launched a concerted attack against a vitally important portion of the United Nations lines, this battalion ... bore the brunt of the assault. ... Heavy casualties were suffered by the men of the battalion as a result of the foe's constant efforts to destroy them, but, even under the most intense fire, they would not quit their positions until their fire mission was completed. ... As a result of the ceaseless and heroic efforts of the personnel of the 461st

Be Happy, Be Free, Dance!

Infantry Battalion (Heavy Mortar), mortar fire alone held back waves of the attackers as the defenders worked desperately to close gaps in their lines caused by the frenzied assaults of the foe. ..."

I was no hero. I received the customary National Defense Service Medal, United Nations and Korean conflict medals, three battle stars for various campaigns, the combat infantryman's badge and the distinguished unit citation. Not every moment was spent facing the enemy. There were even times when life took on a certain semblance of normalcy. I was the only one in our entire battalion to attend a Passover Seder in the City of Chunchon. General Maxwell D. Taylor, Commanding Officer of the Eighth Army, conveyed the following message to us:

"May the ancient struggle of freedom, which the Passover symbolizes, inspire us all to ever increasing devotion to those lofty ideals for which we strive in our day. With faith in God and with the spirit of freedom ever aglow in the hearts of men, we will achieve a world of liberty and peace for all mankind."

Passover at the airport in Chunchon, Korea, 1953

I had a jeep and a driver assigned to me so I made sure that we brought back enough matzo for all the Jewish GIs in my battalion's front line companies for the remainder of the Passover holiday. Our Christian chaplain from Texas - with whom I was very close - took an immense liking to matzo which he had never tasted before. When I sliced up a kosher salami that Aunt Nelly and Uncle Kurt had sent, and served it on bits of matzo, Chaplain Richardson was almost ready to convert.

I became the battalion artist, designing Thanksgiving dinner menus and Christmas holiday cards which we duplicated on mimeograph machines for the men to send home. I also painted directional signs which included the battalion's logo, a fire-spitting dragon holding a bolt of lightning while one of its claws clutched a cannonball. Our motto *"You Call, We Maul"* promoted esprit de corps and reminded us of the reality of our mission.

About halfway through my tour, I flew back to Tokyo for five days of rest and recuperation. After living outdoors in the fields and hills of Korea, Japan was paradise. It is amazing how human beings can make transitions so quickly and easily. I loved Japan and became intrigued with the people, their art and lifestyle. I knew of their heinous crimes during the Second World War but somehow I felt no animosity towards them. There was one moment of anxiety when I was sitting in a barber's chair. As he removed the stubble under my chin with a straight razor, he told me that his son was killed in combat. I have always wondered why he felt it necessary to tell me that, especially when I was so vulnerable. Happily he took no vengeance and I am able to relate this episode.

Korea was a difficult country to be in, due to the war, the total neglect of its cities, and the hardships the population had to endure during so many years of foreign exploitation and occupation. I spent almost eleven months in tents and bunkers on unfriendly, hilly terrain. Our winter was long, snowy and cold, sometimes reaching

Be Happy, Be Free, Dance!

20 degrees below zero, and because of our proximity to enemy lines, we could not build fires for warmth. We had to rise carefully from our sleeping bags to avoid being jabbed by icicles that had formed inside the tent. An anonymous GI wrote a poem called "Oriental Hell" which includes the lines:

> *Below the Manchurian border*
> *Korea is the spot*
> *Where we are doomed to spend time*
> *In a land which God forgot*
>
> *When we get to heaven*
> *St. Peter to the Lord will tell*
> *These are the boys from Korea*
> *They have spent their time in Hell*

The army had a procedure for rotating troops out of the combat zone: they awarded us points toward tickets back home, based on our proximity to the battle line. I was in the "close combat" zone for the entire time in Korea, but replacements were slow in coming during the spring of 1953, so my tour was extended two extra months. Fortunately I got out in June, without a scratch, only weeks before the cease-fire of July 27. I held the rank of staff sergeant, having missed out on a commission because I was not a citizen. About ten days prior to my scheduled departure, the ROK battalion which we were defending came under a surprise attack by Chinese troops hoping to grab some land before the anticipated cease-fire which was to leave each side with the territory they then controlled. The ROK unit quickly became disoriented and they scattered, leaving our men totally exposed. I led an ammunition convoy up the mountain and spent three days under small arms fire, fueled by adrenaline and "No-Doze" pills. Back at Headquarters Company, I was debriefed and I correctly predicted that we could not hold the line.

On June 18, I bade farewell to my buddies. The trucks took us out of the dusty hills, ever further from harm's way. The replacement depot at Inchon was a welcome sight where processing and medical clearance took several days. Semantics aside, the Korean "police action" was a war and not all of us who landed there almost a year earlier were to return home. The flagpole in front of the headquarters building was set in a concrete replica of the Eighth Army insignia, and it had a bronze plaque inscribed:

"Dedicated to those that fought and died so that this flag might fly."

While I was waiting to be evacuated, I learned that my prediction had been correct: the battalion I just left had suffered many casualties while being driven from its position.

On the troop ship Gen. C.C. Ballou, we began our transition back to civilian life. We talked little of our combat experience. We noted the absence of the

At the Tomb of the Unknown Soldier, Arlington National Cemetery, 1953

Kimchi aroma that made C-rations taste like gourmet food. We wondered how it would be to sit on chairs instead of helmets and whether we could talk without having every other word start with the sixth letter of the alphabet. We had to remember what a toilet was and how to flush it. Along with about twenty others, I spent most of the voyage sitting in a lifeboat playing chess. By the time American shores were in sight, a sergeant from Boston and I had triumphed over all challengers but we couldn't best each other.

In Seattle, we were honored with a rainy ticker-tape parade. The army chartered eleven two-engine propeller

Be Happy, Be Free, Dance!

driven planes for those of us from the New York area. Before my flight even took off, three planes had engine trouble and turned back. Having survived Korea, we wondered if there was a hidden message, so some men decided to take the train. The oxygen intake failed briefly on my plane as we were flying over the Rocky Mountains but we got through safely. It was a long trip, before the advent of non-stop, coast to coast flights; we had to refuel in Cheyenne, Wyoming and again in Omaha, Nebraska. After a month-long furlough, I was ordered to Camp Kilmer in New Jersey, where for the next sixty days, I supervised the processing of discharge papers for enlisted personnel. My service in Korea earned me an early release from active duty and on October 30, 1953, three months sooner than the usual two-year requirement, I donned civilian clothes. I was proud to have served my country, to have given something back. I was also thankful to be home safe and happy to be out of uniform. It was time to go forward with my life.

9. Settling Down

During my last few weeks at Camp Kilmer, I wrote a sparse resume, emphasizing my artistic ability. I sent it out to the display directors of the most fashionable specialty stores lining New York's elegant Fifth Avenue. The first positive reply came from Sidney Ring, Director of Visual Merchandising for Saks Fifth Avenue, so I promised to see him as soon as I was discharged. On Monday, November 2, 1953, after only one weekend at home, I met him at his office. Leaning over, he whispered, "I'll pay you forty-five dollars a week, but don't tell anyone. That's more than some of the others are getting." (It was also more than the extra combat compensation I received each month in Korea.) Actually, I probably would have paid him for the chance to work at this flagship store, at the time still revered as the darling of the carriage trade. The busy holiday season for display people was about to start so I reported for work on the day following my interview. I continued doing windows and interiors there for three years while accepting some free-lance business on the side, and that eventually turned into a full-time venture. Though I enjoyed the creativity and freedom, I soon realized its limitations. There was only so much one could charge for installing a window display, no matter how good it was, and working in tight, confined quarters, often lifting and moving cumbersome objects was physically demanding.

When I informed the owner and President of one of my freelance accounts, The Edgar C. Hyman Co., that I intended to give up my business, Mr. Hyman offered me a job. This company manufactured the fashionable "Echo Scarves" and needed a production assistant for their domestic line. When I protested that I knew nothing about manufacturing, he asked me if I could figure out how many yards of 36" wide fabric were needed to produce a dozen 18" squares. Mr. Hyman was impressed with my quick reply of "three yards" and thus started a relationship with the company that lasted thirty-three years.

My social life was typical of the times: attending dances at the Y, double dating, parties, going out for pizza or just "hanging out." During that time, all my close friends had married. Leonard Ginsburg was an artist and a good friend since we met at Camp *Achvah* in 1950. When he married Fran Frost, I was honored to be his best man. Fran's friend, Annette Abraham had attended high school with Sheila Fishbein, a legal assistant with a New York law firm. Somehow her phone number made its way from Annette to Fran to me, and I parked it in my wallet for weeks. When I finally called Sheila on February 13, 1957, I rang up quite a phone bill. We agreed to meet three days later.

I had found my love, my soul mate. Sheila lived in the borough of Queens and I lived in the Bronx, so a long courtship was not affordable. (The toll on the Triboro Bridge was twenty-five cents each way and my new Oldsmobile probably got less than eight miles to the gallon.) But there was never any doubt in my mind that we were meant to spend the rest of our lives together. We talked, we planned and we dreamed. Long before we made any commitment, I found myself saying, "when we are married ..." On September 18, 1957, seven months after our first date, I gave my love an engagement ring.

Sheila later claimed I planned it for that day, which was her birthday, so I wouldn't have to buy a separate gift, and I reminded her that it really was the biggest gift she had ever gotten on her birthday. On December 15, a beautiful Sunday afternoon, Sheila Eileen Fishbein and I were married at the Forest Hills Inn in Queens.

My brother Ernest earned a Bachelor's degree in Business Administration from the City College of New York in January 1958. He joined the Army Reserves – playing on their baseball and softball teams – during a six-month tour that ended in November, 1958. He attended a dance at the 92nd Street Y with a good friend, where they met a couple of girls and decided to toss a coin to determine who would approach which girl. His friend won the toss, but fortunately Ernest wound up with Esther Hutterer whom he married in June, 1959. Ernest and Esther had a good marriage and were blessed with three sons: Michael in February 1961, Gary in November 1963 and Matt in September 1966. Ernest's career started out in advertising and marketing, but he quickly learned that greater rewards could be achieved in the flourishing world of Real Estate. Tragically, Esther died of Hodgkin's-related disease in January 1969. With the help of housekeepers, Ernest was a successful single parent. In December 1969

Sheila and me on our wedding day, December 15, 1957

Be Happy, Be Free, Dance!

Ernest and Doris, Florida, 2005

Ernest's four sons and their families, November 2004

he met the lovely Doris Nadler, who lived in Queens and worked at Lehman Brothers on Wall Street. They fell in love and married in April, 1970. Their son, Neil, was born in June, 1972. Ernest and Doris retired to Florida; they are now grandparents of eight.

Following a brief honeymoon at the Royal York Hotel in Miami Beach, Florida, Sheila and I settled into a charming one-bedroom apartment in the Briarwood section of Queens. We entertained often and spent many happy hours with family and friends. Two-and-a-half years later, on June 7, 1960, our first son arrived. We named him Marc David, for my father. In the spring of

Settling Down

1961, we moved into the ground-floor apartment of a two-family house on 150th Street in Kew Garden Hills. Laurence (Larry), our second son, who was named for my mother, was born on January 29, 1963. Throughout our married life, we formed wonderful, lasting friendships. We were involved in civic and charitable organizations and played active roles in John V. Lindsay's successful 1965 campaign for mayor of New York City.

We purchased a home in Port Washington on Long Island in 1967, and soon became integrated in community life, becoming involved in our synagogue, volunteering with not-for-profit organizations and getting immense satisfaction in return. Here again, we forged great lasting friendships, which richly enhanced our lives. We vacationed, traveled and enjoyed what life had to offer. Both our children grew up and flourished in Port Washington, maturing into fine, sensitive, and caring young men. Marc graduated from Emerson College while Larry attended the University of Pennsylvania in Philadelphia, and graduated from Wharton. He later returned to Penn for his law degree.

Marc David, 2005

In 1983, Sheila and I bought a second home in the foothills of the Berkshires, which served as our escape from the pressures of our careers. (Sheila, who had devoted her energies to our children during their school years and served on numerous boards of not-for-profit organizations, had returned to the business world as sales executive in the handbag industry.) I was still an officer of The Edgar C. Hyman Co. (renamed the Echo Design Group, Inc.), having headed their production, operations, administration and Human Resources. But early retirement had always been my goal. I missed so much by not experiencing a normal childhood and there were so

Be Happy, Be Free, Dance!

Sheila and me, 2003

many things I could not do because of my work-related responsibilities. I left the business world in 1990 and Sheila did likewise a few years later.

Although I attended art school I consider myself basically self-taught. As a member of numerous art associations on Long Island and the Berkshires, I exhibit at juried and membership shows. I have been represented in galleries, sold privately and had my oil paintings hung in museum and corporate settings. Sheila and I both became increasingly more active, giving back to the community. Sheila has been an officer, board member or committee member in many organizations including the National Council of Jewish Women, United Jewish Appeal, the PTA, Friends of the Port Washington Library, the Interfaith Nutrition Network (which provided meals and housing for homeless and abused people on Long Island), North Shore Child and Family Guidance Association and Brandeis Women's Group. I have been involved with some of the same groups, and many Holocaust organization speakers' bureaus. I serve on the board of directors of the Holocaust Memorial and Educational Center of Nassau County. I frequently speak about my experiences and teach the evils of prejudice, intolerance and disrespect for people who are different from us. My special interest in children's welfare has led me to serve on non-profit boards that provide scholarships, loans and mental health care for young people. I occasionally write human-interest stories, opinions and editorial columns for newspapers.

We have two wonderful grandchildren via Larry and our daughter-in-law, Gail. I realized how blessed we were when Arden Danielle Weilheimer, our first grandchild, was born on September 21st, 2000. Reflecting on events of earlier years I realized that I needed to leave a message for her and generations not yet born: "Be Happy, Be Free, Dance!" I wrote the following article which was published in the *Port Washington News*.

Torah mantle, dedicated on Holocaust Remembrance Day 2002, based on my painting

Be Happy, Be Free, Dance!

With Arden Danielle Weilheimer, 2001

Dance, My Precious Arden, Dance!

Arden. Arden Danielle. My granddaughter. At nine months of age, this beautiful, happy little girl does not yet speak but she knows I am her Poppy and she loves to run her tiny fingers through my soft gray beard. As I watch her pressing the buttons on her toy music box to activate the tune of "Mary had a Little Lamb," she wiggles her arms, flexes her knees as if they were bungee cords, and does her own version of a dance. She looks at me for approval as the ends of her sweet little lips stretch towards her ears to form an engaging happy-face smile. Proud of her own accomplishments, she claps her hands and promptly loses her balance. I cry. I cry without shedding tears for this moment of joy.

It was not supposed to be like this. Jewish children were never to be born again. The Nazi's priority was murdering children first. No Jewish children growing up to adulthood meant an end to Jewish civilization. One and half million youngsters were killed - 15 out of 16 children who were trapped in Europe at the onset of hostilities did not live to see the defeat of Germany in World War II. Hitler's concentration camps made me an orphan but fate assigned number 16 to me. I survived. Jewish people survived and regenerated. Little Arden is here in spite of Germany's "final solution to the Jewish question." My precious Arden dances

Settling Down

unaware of the Nazis' heinous crimes committed amid a continent full of eager collaborators and a world of paralyzed bystanders.

Friends alerted me to the indescribable joy of being a grandfather. They were right. It is a feeling that cannot be explained or expressed adequately but must be experienced. My sweet little Arden, you cannot imagine how much happiness you bring to your devoted, loving parents, to Grandee and Poppy and all who know you. You will never really understand the fate of your not-so-far removed ancestors. No one can. It defies comprehension. But know and remember your roots. Blossom, beautiful child. Be happy, be free. Dance!

On January 7, 2003, Arden became the big sister to a beautiful baby boy, Ethan Philip. This blessed occasion prompted me to imagine the festivities taking place in heaven:

Ethan Philip Weilheimer, 2004

Triumph of the Spirits

There was excitement in the air and as I looked up into a clear sky, I could sense the joy and activities taking place in the celestial kingdom. On the eighth day of our grandson's life, we celebrated his bris, the circumcision ritual which denotes the sign of the covenant with the Jewish people. The stars in the firmament glittered that evening, no doubt because of the spiritual energy created by the souls of our departed loved ones as they rejoiced in the heavens above. The Weilheimer, Wetzler, Fishbein and Stern ancestors were all there. Our Ethan's great-Poppy, Philip Fishbein, tended bar, generously filling

Be Happy, Be Free, Dance!

Larry, Ethan, Arden and Gail, 2005

each glass (he used to say "Why make two when one will do?") and "Dee Dee" cut up a spool of red ribbon for bows to ward off the evil spirits.

Great-Nana, Nelly Stern, baked her famous apple shalet and gently coated everyone's favorite almond cake with her traditional mixture of confectioners' sugar and cocoa powder. Great-Poppa Kurt, as usual, struggled to focus his camera to record this happy event. Meanwhile, somewhere in heaven, Great-Oma Lilly played the violin for which she had won public acclaim on earth while Great-Opa Max, denied the pleasure of seeing his sons mature and procreate, sang his favorite song: "Du bist mein augenstern ..." (You are the star of my eye). My own Oma Lina was setting her table for the family dinner while Opa, Cantor Solomon Wetzler, had just put the final stitches on the embroidered linen Wimpel, spelling out Raphael Aaron ben Levy, the Hebrew name for Ethan Philip Weilheimer.

A jubilant congregation of my grandchildren's ancestors celebrated the continuity of the Weilheimer lineage.

10. In Touch with the Past

For years I longed to visit *Mutti's* grave at the cemetery near *Camp de Gurs*. In preparation for visiting France in May 1993, I contacted several people who could facilitate my mission. Oskar Althausen was a Gurs Survivor, who returned to Mannheim, Germany, after the war. He had organized annual pilgrimages to the camp and was thus very familiar with what I could not have remembered but needed to know. He gave me directions and maps and explained what I could expect to see. He pinpointed *Mutti's* resting place in plot #767. When Sheila and I approached the town, we found road signs pointing to the former Camp and the *Cimetière des Déportés* (Cemetery of the Deportees).

In 1945, the "Federation of Jewish Societies for the Basses-Pyrénées" had erected a memorial, but it soon became totally overgrown with weeds. Two years later, groups of Survivors revisited the graves and were distressed by their deteriorated conditions. They discussed the situation with authorities from Baden and the Palatinate where the deceased had originated, and some well-meaning Germans took over care of the cemetery. During the early 1960s they renovated the site, replacing makeshift markers with permanent marble headstones. It will remain under their perpetual care for 99 years. *Mutti's* name was unfortunately misspelled on the headstone, an error I have since corrected. It was good to spend some private moments at this spot and – not having brought a prayer

141

book with me – I recited the *Kaddish* (the Jewish prayer for the dead) in a combination of Hebrew and English to the best of my memory.

Under a shady tree, facing the rows of graves, a tall monument topped by the Star of David, graces this peaceful setting with a mute testimony to human suffering. An inscription proclaims that it was erected "In memory of all the Jews deported to the extermination camps and the 1,250 deceased who rest here, victims of the barbaric Nazis," but of course – as with similar monuments in Europe – there is no mention of the local anti-Semites who were complicit in their deaths. At a caretaker's cottage near the entrance of the cemetery, books and memorabilia about the camp can be purchased.

The site was a mere ghost of a distant past. I stood there, disoriented, with no recollection of where anything had once been. It was surreal. The terrain where so much deprivation and suffering had taken place had morphed into a peaceful benign plateau. My emotions were short-circuited: I could not recall myself as the lice-infected nine-year-old child who was rescued from these grounds by the Quakers fifty-two years earlier. This profane strip of earth had been reclaimed and rehabilitated by nature. Still, I had to go and see it, even though it was alien and I felt detached. We drove on to the town of Navarreux, purchased French bread, cheese and wine, found a charming park and picnicked.

In planning my trip, I had also written to the former orphanage, *La Maison des Pupilles*. In reply, extending an invitation to visit and tour the premises, the director informed me that the building now housed the *Albert Curvale Institute De Reeducation*, a boarding school for children from difficult home environments. I needed to see it.

Nothing looked familiar. I remembered the surroundings, the lush, hilly landscape, which formed the base of the

In Touch with the Past

La Maison des Pupilles, Aspet, around 1940

Pyrénées, but I couldn't even remember if the houses we passed along our way had existed fifty years before. Only the outside of the former orphanage was instantly recognizable, perhaps because I had kept a picture postcard of it for all these years. As I opened the front door, I found myself entering unfamiliar rooms. Everyone on the staff was too young to know that these premises had once been an orphanage. Only one person spoke enough English to give me some basic information. Revisiting this place where I spent sixteen months of my childhood was unsettling. Had it been a dream? Where was Hugo Schiller's bed? Where did Manfred Mayer, Rolf Hess or Karl Landau sleep? What corner held Alice Resch's bed with Ernstele's next to it? Where was I? Where were the beds of those who cried night after night, the youngest ones who could not understand why their parents sent them away? The silent walls did not yield a clue. I left, feeling cheated, yet again. The site did not bring me satisfaction or comfort, or answers to my questions. Nevertheless it was important for me to have been there, to once more see the place that was *La Maison des Pupilles,* even if only to discover that I had no attachment to it.

A similar experience came over me on a subsequent visit to *Yad Vashem* (the Holocaust Authority and Museum in Jerusalem). As I walked through "The Valley of the Communities," where the names of European cities made *Judenrein* had been carved into Jerusalem stones, I came across "Ludwigshafen" and snapped a photo of this stone, the symbol of my birth city, but I felt nothing. Was I too young to have harbored any emotional connection? Was I afflicted with selective amnesia?

Also in 1993, I received a letter from the Mayor of Ludwigshafen, inviting me to visit at their expense. Since 1986 the city had extended a welcome to its former Jewish citizens. The letter stated that I would be escorted around the city, taken to reconstructed landmarks and I could experience life in modern Ludwigshafen. Having long ago promised myself never again to set foot on that contaminated soil, I wrote a letter, stating my lack of interest in the rebuilt city and describing my memory of events during the Third Reich. It seemed dry. There was more I wanted to say but didn't know what it was. The letter remained on my desk for weeks until I decided to add a postscript saying I would make the trip if I could have a platform at a university or take part in a panel discussion where I could speak of my Holocaust experience with German people who lived through the Nazi era. About a month later, I received a reply, outlining the various itineraries previous groups of returnees had followed. They had been taken to the Jewish this, the Jewish that or the former site of the Jewish ... My request for engagement was ignored so I declined the offer. Cynically, I felt that their invitation was motivated more by the younger generation's desire for closure on Germany's collective guilt than a sincere effort to acknowledge or even comprehend their nation's atrocities towards its former Jewish citizens. They needed us to exorcise the ghosts of a dark past.

To my knowledge, there is only one Weilheimer in the United States, perhaps in the world, not directly related to me. Harry Weilheimer nevertheless resembles my late uncles and comes from a city near Ludwigshafen. I had met Harry in the early 1990's but even though he lived nearby, we had little contact. Over lunch in July 1996, Harry told me he was about to go to Europe. The following week in Switzerland, he attended a gathering where he met Hanna Meyer-Moses. She repeated the name and asked, "Do you know any other Weilheimers in America?" "There are a few," Harry replied. "By any chance, did you ever hear of a Richard Weilheimer who has a brother Ernst?" "Yes, as a matter of fact I just had lunch with Richard," Harry said. After confirming our identity, Hanna revealed that she too had been a child at *Camp de Gurs* and *La Maison des Pupilles* and had been looking for us for many years. "It means so much to us when, after such a long time we locate former comrades and can learn of their destiny."

Hanna, four years my senior, was one of the oldest children in the orphanage and over the years, had tried to find the others. She sent me a list of our "brothers and sisters" whom she had located and the address of Alice Resch, the "Quaker Lady, the Angel of Aspet." I had little desire to contact any of the Survivors on the list. It had been 54 years since we last saw each other. I had long forgotten some names, others were familiar, and I could still recall the faces of a few. But I was interested in Alice Resch (now, Alice Resch Synnestvedt) who by then had lived for many years in Copenhagen, Denmark. While we were at *La Maison des Pupilles,* she seemed to have been everywhere when she was needed, but over the years she became the mere shadow of a modest guardian whose name and identity had, at the time of distress, not really mattered. Though she deserved a great deal of gratitude and love, emotional defenses had prevented me from attaching myself to anyone. There was no permanency or security. I had been hurt too often. As I wrote to her, I wondered if our "Angel" would still remember me.

Alice was approaching her 88th birthday and losing her eyesight, but her mind was as sharp as a youngster's. Her memory for details was spectacular. She remembered everything and everyone. More important, Alice had written a journal and kept photographs to communicate with her deaf mother, and later she donated her eyewitness account of *Camp de Gurs* and the orphanage to *Yad Vashem*, and The United States Holocaust Memorial Museum in Washington, DC. Alice sent me copies of some photos, pointing out Ernst and me and the other children. When I wrote that I had only a scant memory of her she replied: "that you do not remember me is very natural. Your life was so filled with new impressions and so very serious for a little boy who was suddenly left alone, cut away from the security of a happy home and parents."

Each of Alice's "children" lost contact with her upon our rescue from Europe. The oceans we crossed freed us and simultaneously severed us from our former lives, and then we had to adjust to our adopted countries and environments. We no longer had contact with our parents. None of us could possibly have understood the Holocaust or what we had so narrowly escaped. We had not yet realized Alice's role, nor could we, as children have appreciated it. Almost four decades later, Uri (formerly Karl) Landau, who was living in Israel, wondered whether any of the Quaker ladies from Toulouse were still alive. Research led to Alice and Helga Holbek, her supervisor and friend, both of whom were living in Denmark. Uri contacted Menachem (formerly Manfred) Mayer, Ruth Berman Gogol and George Basnizki, all in Israel, and they soon re-established steady contact with the two women. Alice's four Israeli "children" presented documents and testimonies about the rescue work in France to the committee on the "Righteous Among the Nations" at *Yad*

Vashem. In 1983, at the Israeli Embassy in Copenhagen, Alice and Helga were presented with the much-deserved medal. By coincidence and word of mouth other "children" from France, Switzerland, England and the United States, had found Alice as well. Seven of them, along with spouses and children, hosted a reunion in Israel the following year, when Alice was invited to a tree-planting ceremony that honored her and Helga. Unfortunately, Helga had died a few months before, so Alice made the trip alone. Each of the "children" in attendance shoveled some fertile soil over the trees' roots, and a brass plaque naming "the righteous" was set next to each sapling. The event was covered by Scandinavian and German newspapers.

Alice Resch Synnestvedt's plaque at Yad Vashem's "Avenue of the the Righteous," 1988

When I contacted Alice in 1996, I also got in touch with Hugo Schiller, my friend from Gurs, Aspet and the Maccabi athletic club, who was by then living in Myrtle Beach, South Carolina. In her first letter to me, Alice suggested that I contact Kurt Wagner (formerly Walker) who had been in Gurs, Aspet and on the *Nyassa* with us. I phoned Kurt in Illinois and we started writing and exchanging videos made for Steven Spielberg's *Shoah Foundation*.

In 1997, Sheila attended a book discussion at a Jewish Community Center on Long Island. At the end of the program, she suggested a Holocaust-related book for the next discussion. One of the other women asked Sheila why she chose that particular title. "My husband is a Survivor," Sheila answered. "So am I," came the reply. Additional questions were asked: "Where was he from ... Where was he sent to ... and then where?" Each answer was followed by "So was I." Thus I found another child from Gurs and Aspet: Eva Herz Boden.

At a seminar I was giving to a group of teachers and parents at the Holocaust Memorial and Educational Center in Glen Cove, New York, a young lady sitting in the first row became very restless. She seemed to be familiar with my story. When I spoke of Gurs and *La Maison des Pupilles*, she exclaimed "Oh my God, my father and uncle were there too." Thus I learned the whereabouts of Frederick Raymes (formerly Manfred Mayer) of Florida and his brother, Menachem Mayer, who lives in Israel.

I was invited to attend the dedication ceremony of the Museum of Jewish Heritage – A Living Memorial to the Holocaust, in New York. Ann Shore, President of The Hidden Child Foundation/ADL was sitting next to me. She invited me to one of their speaker's workshops. At that meeting, we were asked to introduce ourselves and give a few details about our experience. Here was yet another surprise: on my right was Karl Haussman. He and his older brother Gunther were among the fifty children from Gurs originally chosen for *La Maison des Pupilles*. Karl backed out at the last minute, choosing to remain with his parents while Gunther went to Aspet with us. In September 1942, Gunther got special permission to visit his parents who had been transferred to Rivesaltes.

Unfortunately, the Vichy authorities wouldn't let him out again, but shipped him with his parents to a transit camp just northeast of Paris. On September 11, 1942 they were loaded onto the infamous cattle cars of convoy #31 at Drancy and sent to Auschwitz where they perished. But Karl, who had originally remained with his parents, escaped from *Camp de Gurs* and hid in France for the duration of the war. Each one of my "brothers and sisters" from Aspet has a unique story. Some survived by hiding with "Righteous Gentiles" or in safe houses, convents, or monasteries. Some were smuggled over the borders into Spain or Switzerland, while others like me managed to get on a boat out of Europe. Gunther Haussman was the only one of the forty-eight of us who did not survive.

Another Survivor who wanted to retrace her whereabouts during the Holocaust was planning to take her family to Europe but didn't remember much about where she had been. On a visit to New York, she came to the Holocaust Memorial and Educational Center of Nassau County to do some research. She remembered being in an orphanage in Aspet but was not sure of the name. When my picture and background came up on the computer screen, she was delighted to find that I was an active volunteer at the Center. Within the hour I was reunited with Ruth Reinhold Rosenberg of Florida. And so this small world phenomenon keeps occurring.

Hugo and I had wanted to do something for Alice's 90th birthday in 1998. She had recently moved, and given up most of her possessions. Hugo suggested that we bring her to the United States for a birthday celebration and reunion. She was no longer able to travel by herself so we invited her friend, Aase Ingerslev, who was editing Alice's journals for publication, to accompany her. Alice and Aase arrived in Myrtle Beach in December. Hugo, Eve, Ernest and I were joined by Ruth David, whose brother Michel Oppenheimer was an Aspet child now living in Paris, and Al Sperber who was hidden in a monastery through

Alice's persuasive determination. Her joy at meeting those who survived mostly due to her efforts, their spouses, children and grandchildren, was an indescribable emotional experience for everyone. For most of a week we celebrated life, and despite Alice's modesty, her heroism in rescuing so many children. This righteous person let her humanity and selflessness motivate whatever she did because it was "the right thing to do." Period! She refused any other explanation.

A reporter from *The Sun News* of Myrtle Beach, South Carolina was assigned to follow us around and CNN's "Headline News" reported our activities nightly. The television crew for "Good Morning America" spent a day taping our celebrations and remembrances. Mayors and other dignitaries paid tribute to Alice, and she was presented with the keys to Conway and Myrtle Beach. The Rotary Club honored her with a luncheon where Hugo and I spoke of the Holocaust and Alice's role in it. The local *Chabad* (Lubavitcher Jewish movement) invited Alice to light the Chanukah menorah as the rabbi declared "When you light a candle, it chases the darkness away." I spoke of my dilemma, during the weeks prior to her arrival, as I was trying to devise some way to thank Alice. How could I show my appreciation to a person who did so much to save my life? I concluded that the only way is to lead a commendable life, to instill ethical values in my own children, and to urge them to live their lives to the fullest. But I want them to always remember that their existence was possible because of Alice Resch Synnestvedt. Ancient rabbinical writings state "One who saves one life saves the world." Alice saved the world.*

The Aspet "children" spent many hours talking about our inability to fathom what happened to us during those

---

* For the complete story of Alice Resch Synnestvedt, the "Aspet Children" and other efforts to rescue Jews from the Nazis, see: *Over the Highest Mountains; A Memoir of Unexpected Heroism in France during WWII*, published by Intentional Productions, 2005.

years and we recalled incidents that etched lasting impressions into our young minds. We spoke of the good memories that gave us impetus and strength to assume normal lives. Spending her 90th birthday with "her children" was an exciting time for Alice, but it also gave us an opportunity to acknowledge her role and express our appreciation and gratitude. Even the nostalgia was important, as we re-connected with comrades and events that played such an important part in our young lives. Alice had not been to the United States in sixty years and she wanted to see New York City once again. It was beautiful with Christmas lights and the traditional tree in its splendor at the Rockefeller Center ice skating rink. Alice was delighted when Sheila and I drove her and Aase through New York's Midtown, Greenwich Village, Soho, the Westside and the Eastside and she was thrilled by the United Nations. Although poor eyesight robbed Alice of the architectural details and the people bedecked in holiday glitter, she could see the outlines of the buildings and feel the spirit and tempo of New York. Everyone was tired as we sat down for dinner at a quaint little restaurant near Gramercy Park. But when I asked Alice if she would like white or red wine with her meal, this perky ninety year old replied: "I have to look at the menu first and choose what I'm going to eat."

Alice and Aase stayed in the City overnight rather than make the commute to our suburban home. Sheila and I met our guests for breakfast the next morning and our eldest son Marc joined us at the hotel to greet Alice. What a thrill it was for her to meet him! Our next stop was the US Holocaust Memorial Museum in Washington, DC where Alice had donated many of her photographs and her name is inscribed on the wall of the "Righteous Among the Nations." The Director of Survivors' Affairs, Martin Goldman, greeted us and within minutes, dozens of high school students surrounded Alice, asking questions. Thus, we personalized the Nazis' heinous crimes and brought them into a sharp focus. Alice insisted

Be Happy, Be Free, Dance!

that she did nothing to deserve the attention and honors. She kept repeating: "I only did my job." But giving aid to a Jew could have led to summary execution or at best, deportation to a concentration camp. In her modesty Alice asserted: "There were others." Yes, there certainly were, yet Alice was not the commanding officer operating from behind the lines; she was in the trenches, in harm's way. She fought for "her children."

Perhaps the most touching display at the Museum is the heap of shoes. There are unfashionable shoes of peasants and the elderly, shoes of the young and newlyweds, and shoes of toddlers barely old enough to walk, work shoes and dress shoes. It is only a small sample of the hundreds of thousands of pairs of shoes gathered from those who were murdered so we can speculate forever about the identity and lives of the people from whom they were plundered. Where did they come from? Had we known them? Where had those shoes taken them along life's way in happier times? The shoes symbolize their owners' unrealized dreams, their violently snuffed-out lives. Imagine where these shoes might have led ... the young children, the toddlers, who might have become doctors, scientists, inventors and artists. How many diseases might have been conquered? What would they have contributed to humanity and how would our world have been changed? We were very pleased that our son Larry, and daughter-in-law Gail, traveled to Washington to spend some time with Alice. Larry asked "How were you able to get my father out of the camp and to the orphanage?" Alice, with her characteristic wit and modesty replied: "by train of course." Over dinner that evening, we gave Alice two books from the Holocaust Museum: one was appropriately entitled "The World Must Know" and the other was about the heroic Scandinavians who rescued Jews.

I have often wondered if I would have the courage and strength to do what she did. I certainly hope so, but the crucial test comes only when one is faced with life's trying situations. Alice passed the test. Her name had surely earned its place on that wall among others who had not lost their humanity, those who were not immobilized.

Hal Myers (formerly Hans Hanauer) is another Aspet "child" now living in Ohio, who had been searching for Alice for several years after experiencing a need to learn more about his past. Two years after our reunion, he was successful in locating her. When Alice told him of our 1998 get-together, he contacted me and other Survivors from Gurs and Aspet. We planned another reunion with Alice in August 2002 in Copenhagen, Denmark. Aase and her husband Per Ingerslev very generously offered their lovely home in the Copenhagen suburb of Fredensborg, for our get-together.

I had not seen them for sixty years: Georg Basnizki, Uri Landau, Alfred Stein, Suse Moses, Hal Myers, Michel Oppenheimer. We came from the United States, Israel, France, Switzerland and Germany. Some of us brought our spouses. We were joined by Michel's sister Ruth David (who escaped the Nazi terror via the *kindertransport* to England) and Ann Kunish, a Norwegian-American who had just completed translating Alice's journals into English. Our reunion was low-keyed, filled with luncheons, dinners and a lot of good conversation. We each remembered something others had long forgotten and we toasted Alice with praise for what she had done. There was a unique bond among us seven. A reporter for Copenhagen's leading newspaper covered our reunion for its Sunday Magazine section.

With Alice Resch Synnestvedt in Copenhagen, August 2002

Aase and Per took Sheila and me on an interesting side trip to the small waterfront village of Dragoer to learn about the Danish rescuers who smuggled Jewish citizens to safety. When the Nazis occupied Denmark in the spring of 1940, the Danes refused to carry out Hitler's anti-Jewish policies. Even the Lutheran church declared "Whenever Jews are persecuted as such on racial or religious grounds, the Christian church is duty bound to protect against this action ..." Aase's father, Ib Frederik Freuchen, was a physician, so he could obtain scarce petrol for the car which he used to shuttle Jews from Dragoer to Humleback, where the distance across the sound to Sweden is shorter. Fishing vessels were standing by, waiting to take them on their treacherous journey past German patrol boats. Almost all of Denmark's 7,500 Jews were saved. Who said, "But we didn't know?" Who said, "There was nothing that we could do?"

11. My Mission, My Command

People are the product of their genes, their environment and their life experiences. Most of us Survivors were resilient and rose above the adversity of our earlier experiences. Others spent years dealing with psychic wounds. I attribute much of the psychological stability of our group to the camaraderie and support we gave each other in Aspet. The structure of the orphanage, even during those uncertain and dangerous days, also gave us some semblance of order and humanity. I was able to distract and distance myself from the past and function well in my transplanted life because my Americanization process started early, thanks to my young age, the love and caring of Aunt Nelly and Uncle Kurt, my schooling and subsequent service in the army. I don't know whether to attribute my particular quirks, insecurities and habits to my German cultural origin or to traumatic experiences during the years of Nazi persecution, but I suspect that many in the Survivor community have similar behaviors.

For example, I seldom show my emotions. Friends and relatives have described my reaction to certain events as "numbness." It is not easy for me to laugh and almost impossible to cry but I do both, mostly internally, privately. My cravings for roots, security and comfort cause me to collect things and keep them in accustomed, set places. Safeguarding my home is very important, almost obsessive. I am cautious about establishing relationships; trust must be earned and once connections are made I am always afraid of separation or losing a loved one. It hurts to see food wasted. I grew up hearing about those "starving children in Europe" and cannot forget that I was one of them. I have a hard time discarding perfectly good clothing, just because it is not fashion. For a long time I was nervous when a policeman walked by me and I would tremble when I spotted a squad car. I had to learn that in a free society the police protect law-abiding citizens, a departure from a world where laws are made in the interest of dictators and to support their government's policies. I take comfort in knowing where I'm going and how to get there. Getting lost invokes memories of being isolated and left behind. I have lost lots of sleep over some events. The 1962 Cuban missile crisis – when our country faced-off against the Soviet Union over the clandestine placement of missiles ninety miles from our shores – caused me great internal turmoil. I came very close to giving up all I had worked for in order to relocate my family to a safer part of the country. I did not again want to ignore the "handwriting on the wall." I kept thinking of that haunting question: "Why didn't your family leave?"

Holocaust Survivors are good citizens. Freedom, safety and opportunities in our adoptive land means more to us than to many native-born who take these "rights" for granted. Having experienced discrimination, persecution and abuse, we speak out against injustice. We vote, pay our taxes and volunteer for civic and charitable causes. We practice and teach tolerance and respect for minorities. We are law abiding and pray that no Holocaust Survivor's name appears in a newspaper in connection with a crime. We are proud to be Americans and fiercely dedicated to our country. We acknowledge that our survival was mostly due to luck. We acquired defense mechanisms that remain with us, so we are always alert to innuendos and impending dangers. We are also suspicious. We are prepared to survive again. We always need to know where the emergency exists are located.

But why didn't I talk about my experiences? I wasn't trying to deny them, but there were many reasons to filter out what was concealed in memory before it reached my lips. For years few of us ever spoke of our "previous" lives. The unspeakable events of the Holocaust challenged our ability to communicate them. At the time of my immigration to the United States, and even after the allied victory, we were confronted with utter disbelief when we attempted to tell about our experiences. Nothing made me angrier or more likely to recoil into that protected cocoon of silence than the terrible nagging question: "Why didn't your family just leave?"

For years, when I heard such naïve challenging queries, I was unprepared and ignorant of the obstacles facing European Jews. I was embarrassed and ashamed that my family did not have the foresight to uproot themselves from their ancestral soil of Germany when it became so hostile. I was a child, unable to grasp the situation, unaware of the politics and historical events. I groped for answers and wrestled with the question of why I survived, until I understood that I need not carry any guilt.

There were many reasons for maintaining my silence. Everyone in our German-Jewish community in Washington Heights lost family members, friends or former neighbors and it was painful to bring it up. We had not yet benefited from the distance of time, that element which may not heal but puts a buffer zone between the present and past, and allows us to absorb a tragedy. The relatively small number of us who reached the shores of America were thankful to our adopted country, so we wanted to avoid accusations and confrontations out of political consideration and the ever-present fear of anti-Semitic backlash. The American public, having suffered and sacrificed to win the "Great War," was jubilant in its victory. It had not yet known of, much less understood the "Final Solution" and few people had the patience to listen to stories by immigrant Jews. In my early years, I chose not to expose my memories, but to go forward, always conscious of my past, but able to will it into the refuge of silence. I wanted to lead a normal life, so I worked to create a happy and healthy future. The scars were there, but they were benign and I would not let them interfere with my desire to protect my family, especially my children.

Decades later, Winston Churchill referred to the systematic mass slaughter of the Jews as the "crime without a name." Later it became "The Holocaust," a term that means devastating destruction. Eventually, those of us who had experienced those horrible events were referred to as Survivors: "Holocaust Survivors." We suddenly commanded respect as a primary source of history and our audience not only listened to us but demanded scholarly contributions. The world now calls upon Survivors as object lessons – in tolerance training.

We child Survivors are the last living group of witnesses. We were the youngest, the most vulnerable and a prime target for immediate extinction. We were to be denied the hope of a future, the continuity of Jewish generations. Now, as we become aware of our own aging and mortality, we are even more conscious of the fact that our parents never had the opportunity to attain our advanced age. I realized that an accounting of my life experiences would be a precious heritage to bestow on my descendants. So it became our duty to speak for those whose voices were stilled, and all the family trees that would never bear fruit. We must honor and remember them. Equally, we must celebrate the remarkable determination, resiliency and rejuvenation of those who came out alive. We can no longer be silent.

Many Survivors can give testimony, whether they lived through a death camp, a labor camp, a ghetto or spent the war in hiding. Some took on a fake identity or were on the run, evading the Nazis and their collaborators. Others escaped in 1939, 1941 or 1944, or managed somehow to stay alive in Europe until liberation. There are tens of thousands of stories and no two are exactly alike. We are a diminishing lot, suddenly in demand to tell about our experiences and teach our young. We do not wish or deserve to be on a pedestal. We were not heroes, but ordinary, terrified people.

In the mid 1980's, my Rabbi, Martin Rozenberg, one of the few people who knew about my background, asked me to be on a panel discussing the Holocaust experience at an adult education program presented at Paul D. Schreiber High School in Port Washington. I recalled that I went through the entire public school system without ever having heard anything about the Holocaust. That was the first time I opened up, still somewhat guarded, to that part of my life. It was to remain the only time for several more years.

My silence ended abruptly and dramatically on November 9, 1988. The Community Synagogue of Port Washington, of which I was a member, held an evening service to commemorate the 50th anniversary of *Kristallnacht*. Rabbi Rozenberg was on a sabbatical and neither the associate rabbi nor anyone who planned that evening was aware that I had experienced that infamous day, half a century earlier. Sitting in the congregation listening to a visiting speaker, I could hardly contain myself. I broke out in a sweat and felt my heart pounding. I needed to speak. As soon as the invited guest finished his talk, I made my way to the *bimah* and informed the Rabbi that I needed to share my own story of that day's event. The featured speaker and I came from nearby cities and had similar, yet different experiences in 1938, but we had been deported on the very same train to *Camp de Gurs* on October 22, 1940. I spoke for about 40 minutes as the saga of my earlier life came flowing out, released from its self-imposed bondage. It was the turning point which finally ended my silence and compelled me to bear witness in front of the world.

Be Happy, Be Free, Dance!

That evening gave me the opening which allowed me to reconcile with my past. What subsequently started out as occasional requests to speak at schools, civic organizations and synagogues, became more frequent and demanding. The floodgates had now swung open and just as speaking out had been impossible for so long, remaining silent now became impossible. Undeclared testimony was no longer an acceptable option. The more I spoke, the more it became a passion. I knew I had to communicate how the Holocaust evolved from prejudice and hatred into genocide. Speaking and teaching became my mission, a mandate that required me to reach a younger generation.

Innocent people had their lives cut short. Some buried diaries and documents in the sewers beneath their ghetto prisons. They wanted Survivors to know what happened so that future generations would be informed. They were murdered, and many had no surviving family to remember or mourn for them. As attack dogs drove them to the extermination chambers, they pleaded: "Let the world know!" "Do not forget us!" "See and remember!" Their ashes were efficiently spewed out of the chimneys of the death factories. Their remains were scattered in unmarked ravines and invisible graves. Our collective memories are their only tombstones, and I, a Survivor, had an obligation, a sacred command.

The immoral dimension of the *Shoah* has to be communicated, especially in the schools. Aging witnesses must transmit their memories to young people so that they, in turn, may survive the Survivors. That is how we shed light on this period of darkness. We are obligated to tell our stories, to satisfy the last will and testament of those so brutally murdered. But we must also convey the humanity of the victims, for they were not simply the sickly, dying skeletal images, so often depicted. They were not the diseased or vermin infested zombie-like figures their eager executioners reduced them to prior to their slaughter. This is not who they were. They were happy, healthy people. That is how we should remember them.

Now, whenever I speak in a classroom, I discuss the opportunities to make the right choices, to maintain vigilance and to take measures that prevent genocide. The Holocaust was initially made possible by the silence and apathy of Germany's citizens and later, by an impotent, uncaring world. But people like us also allowed Auschwitz to happen. The indifference of free people plays into the hands of evildoers. We cannot be innocent; we cannot be excused for ignoring atrocities that occur within our sight or our knowledge. This is the message that needs to get out, to reach the younger generations, our torchbearers. They also share our responsibilities for remembering the resisters and rescuers, those who had a choice and the courage to act on their conscience. We must learn from this dismal past so that we can make a difference in the future, especially after the Survivor community passes on. Hopefully we can contribute to a more humane society.

When students hear a Holocaust Survivor speak and realize that he or she has a human face much like their own, it has a stronger impact than what they might obtain from a history book. In a confusing modern world, one still threatened by acts of terror, school children must learn how Survivors faced life with courage and determination. They must learn how we were able to put our lives together again, to create families and in most cases, succeed in our endeavors. My friend and Holocaust Survivor, David Gewirtzman, also speaks often to students. He recently ended a talk with lips quivering. Emotionally drenched, he was barely able to blurt out his message: "Someone forgot to write the eleventh commandment: Thou shall not hate!"

The students I reach are remarkable, bright youngsters, of various religions, races and ethnic backgrounds, who attend public, private and parochial schools. In discussions following my talk, I am asked: "With all that happened to you and your family, do you still believe in God?" and "If you could confront Hitler, what would you say to him?" An Orthodox Jewish teenager asked, "The Rabbis teach us that when the Messiah comes, all our dead ancestors will be resurrected. Does that mean Hitler will return?" Some want to know if I ever returned to Germany and how I feel about the German people today.

There is a story about a young German who noticed the blue number tattooed on an Auschwitz Survivor's arm and declared "I too have a tattoo, right on my forehead." "What are you talking about?" the Survivor asked. "Don't you see the swastika above my eyes?" was the reply. Seeing nothing, the former death camp inmate inquired: "Are you pulling my leg?" "No, not at all" the youth answered. "You see, as soon as people realize I'm German, they see me as a Nazi." I tell the students that we who suffered from prejudice must not condemn the innocent. The Holocaust must forever be remembered but our focus should not be misdirected. Although some present-day Germans are willfully ignorant and they refuse to come to terms with their forebears' unforgivable atrocious acts, I assure the students that I do not believe that guilt is inherited. People who have no personal connection to an event, who were not yet born when it occurred, cannot be accused of complicity or bear responsibility for it.

As I look around a typical classroom, I point out that very few fit the "Aryan" mold, the dictator's obsessive vision of a pure super race. By the war's end the Nazis had murdered two out of every three Jews in Europe. I ask the students: "If he had succeeded in annihilating all the Jews, what do you think Hitler would have done with those death factories? Do you think he would have dismantled the camps? What minority group would have been targeted next for extermination?" I urge the students to contemplate the words of the German Lutheran Pastor, Martin Niemoeller, who was arrested by the Gestapo and sent to the Dachau concentration camp, in 1938. He survived, and was liberated by the allies seven years later.

My Mission, My Command

I Didn't Speak Up

In Germany, the Nazis first came for the communists, and I didn't speak up because I wasn't a communist. Then they came for the Jews, and I didn't speak up because I wasn't a Jew. Then they came for the trade unionists, and I didn't speak up because I wasn't a trade unionist. Then they came for the Catholics, and I didn't speak up because I was a Protestant. Then they came for me, and by that time there was no one left to speak for me.

I have also had interesting experiences with adult audiences. A group of Franciscan Friars held a retreat near the Holocaust Memorial and Educational Center in Glen Cove, and found our facilities quite by accident. When I offered to give them a quick tour and background information on the Holocaust, Brother Jacob said that they only had a few minutes to spare. Two hours later we were still talking and I sensed that we were bonding. It was important to them that I forgive the Nazi perpetrators. I led the group into a room where they could see images of the killing ravines, the ovens, the stacks of emaciated, tortured souls and results of bestial medical experimentations performed on human beings. "This I can never forgive," I vowed. As they left, each of the twelve men gave me a bear hug and Brother Lawrence presented me with a religious medallion. Some of them have been back several times, intent on their mission to have me forgive.

Conducting classes shortly after the September 11, 2001 terrorist attacks on the World Trade Center and other targets was particularly difficult. I wondered what interest the atrocities and incomprehensible events of 60 years ago could possibly have for twenty-first century youths, or even their parents, in light of the destruction and impact of that tragedy? Allowing myself to be paralyzed by shock and disbelief, I became addicted to the television coverage of the carnage. I wanted to believe that this was another "War of the Worlds," a hoax, a bad dream, a Hollywood horror film, computerized imagery, or a sick action-video. When reality set in, my eternal optimism dimmed once again and hope became another casualty as murderous hate seized the day. My old wounds were sensitized. Through the scars of my own affliction, I saw the similarities inherent in this evil attack. In desperation, relatives and friends of the missing thousands at the Twin Towers made their way through the rubble circulating photos and descriptions of their loved ones. They searched in hospitals, communication and command centers and they checked the survivor listings on bulletin boards.

At the end of World War II, those of us who had survived the ghettos and concentration camps, made similar inquiries. We too searched for missing relatives by submitting their descriptions and biographies to various agencies – we didn't have photographs! Then too, we waited in vain, clinging to the slightest sliver of hope for those who would never be found. Once again, grieving families had no remains to bury, only mountains of ashes to reflect on. Soon after September 11, newspapers started publishing short accounts of the victims' abbreviated lives and their destroyed families. In shameful and senseless acts of mass murder, we must remember every single precious life lost. There were marked differences as well. The heroic, selfless actions by the New York City firefighters and police in the Twin Towers contrasted starkly with the behavior of German firemen who stood idly by on that 1938 "Night of Broken Glass," as synagogues throughout Nazi Germany burned to the ground and the police egged the hooligans on. Approximately 3,000 lives were lost in the attack on the World Trade Center. Imagine a September eleventh *every day* for 2,000 consecutive days – *nearly five and a half years*. Then visualize the loss of six million murdered Jews.

I believe the message we convey makes a difference. I will fulfill my mission, my command. I will remember not to let the world forget.

12. *Appendix*

Chronology of events in my life and the historical realities that shaped it

January 1941 letter from Opa to his son-in-law in New York

August 1941 letter from the AFSC in Toulouse to headquarters in Philadelphia

Letters from Papi, Mutti and Oma to me and Ernst at *La Maison des Pupilles*

Eulogy for Mutti, Lilly Weilheimer, Gurs July 20, 1941

Be Happy, Be Free, Dance!

A very personal chronology of events in my life and the historical realities that shaped it

1852		The Weilheimers settled in Ludwigshafen, Germany
1898 - 1910		Grandfather Seligman Weilheimer serves as first Jewish City Counselor
WW1		Five Weilheimer brothers serve in the Kaiser's army
1916	September 3	*Papi's* brother (Richard) killed in action at the Somme
1931	November 21	I was born in Ludwigshaven and named for my fallen uncle
1933	January 30	Hitler appointed Chancellor of Germany
1935	September 15	Anti-Jewish racial laws enacted at Nuremberg
1935	December 11	Ernst born in Mannheim
1937		*Mutti's* sisters Nelly and Alice and their husbands leave Germany for the US
1938	July 6	Evian Conference on the problem of Jewish refugees
	November 9-10	*Kristallnacht; Papi* taken to Dachau concentration camp
1938	November	My Jewish school forced to close
1939	February	Senator Robert Wagner's bill to admit 20,000 refugee children dies in committee
	May 13	SS St. Louis leaves Hamburg; over 900 refugees denied entry to Cuba and U.S.
	September 1	Hitler invades Poland; WWII begins
1940	June 22	France capitulates to Hitler; is divided into "occupied" and "Vichy" zones
	October 22	My family and approximately 6,500 others deported from Germany to *Camp de Gurs*
	November	*Mutti,* believing the lie of "resettlement" expresses hope for the future in a poem
1941	February	Ernst and I among 48 children negotiated out of Gurs to the orphanage *La Maison des Pupilles* in Aspet by the Quakers

Appendix

	March	Encouraging letters from *Papi* & *Mutti* begin arriving at Aspet
	March	*Mutti* placed in infirmary
	July 17	*Mutti* dies at Gurs
1942	January 20	Wannsee Conference adopts "Final Solution to the Jewish Problem"
	June 25	Ernst and I depart from Marseilles for the US on the last ship out
	June 30	Adolf Eichmann orders implementation of the "final solution" in France
	July 7	First deportations from Gurs to the death camps
	July 12	We depart Casablanca aboard the SS *Nyassa*
	July 29	We arrive in Baltimore
	August	*Papi's* brother Muni deported to Auschwitz
	August	We meet our aunts Nelly and Alice in New York
	September	I start school at PS 152
	September 22	*Papi's* last letter from Gurs
1943	February 26	*Papi* shipped from Gurs to Drancy
	March 4	*Papi*, his brother Ludwig and sister-in-law Tilde arrive at Sobibor, and are assumed to have been murdered on arrival
1944	June 6	D-Day – the Allies land at Normandy
	December 2	My *Bar Mitzvah*
1947	May 24	Oma dies in the US
1948		I tryout for the US Olympic soccer team
1950	June	My graduation from George Washington High School in New York
	June 25	Start of the Korean War
1952	January 31	I report for induction into the US Army
	July 29	I land at Inchon, Korea exactly ten years after arriving in America
1953	October 30	I return to civilian life

167

Be Happy, Be Free, Dance!

1957	February 16	I meet Sheila Eileen Fishbein
	December 15	We are married at the Forest Hills Inn
1960	June 7	Marc David Weilheimer is born
1963	January 29	Laurence Weilheimer is born
1967		We move to Port Washington, New York
1990	May 31	I retire from the fashion accessory industry
1993	May	Sheila and I make a pilgrimage to Gurs and Aspet
1996	August	I locate my rescuer, Alice Resch Synnestvedt, in Denmark
1998	December	Ernest and I meet with Alice and her "children" from Gurs and Aspet in Myrtle Beach, SC
2001	September 21	Arden Danielle Weilheimer, our first grandchild, is born
2002	August	Another reunion with Alice and other survivors in Copenhagen
2003	January 7	Ethan Philip Weilheimer, our grandson is born

Appendix

Letter from Opa to Kurt, his son-in-law in New York

Mannheim January, 29, 1941

My dear ones:

I don't need to tell you how much I enjoyed the warmth of your letters which I received yesterday. Your wish of course is also mine and that of all our loved ones, from whom, thank God, I get satisfactory reports. I hope it will work out that mother will be able to join Uncle Joseph until her emigration is possible. I do not know why Lilly's low quota number has not yet been called. For the last few days, with the permission from currency control and customs, it has been possible to send parcels of up to 5 kilograms from the Palatinate. I have used this opportunity to send 2 packages, one each to Lilly and mother. However, it is forbidden to send any mail directly or indirectly to enemy territory. I hope mother will realize this and not be worried by my silence.

You wrote that you mailed <u>our</u> papers to Marseilles, but <u>mine</u> should have been sent to <u>Stuttgart</u> and <u>only the papers for mother should have been sent to Marseilles.</u> I urge you to rectify this <u>immediately</u>; otherwise I shall have to wait longer, as numbers up to 30,000 might be called up in Stuttgart. As you know, I am well, thank God.

How are your parents, dear Kurt?

Warm regards and kisses from your loving father.

American Friends Service Committee
16 Boulevard Bonrepos
Toulouse

August 14, 1941

John F. Rich
American Friends Service Committee
20 South 12th Street
Philadelphia U.S.A.

Dear John Rich,

The Marseilles Office sent me a copy of your letter ... concerning the camp feeding scheme, as it is mostly the Toulouse Office who visits the camps, specially: Gurs, Noé, Récébédou and Vernet. ... All those who work in the camps agree that it would be a catastrophe and would mean much misery and many deaths if we would discontinue our feeding scheme. It is of course quite true that <u>officially</u> the camp population gets the same rations as the French civilians but practically they do not even get the official rations. Also it is easily forgotten that all the civilians can buy extra things outside the rations, otherwise they would definitely be undernourished. This is the reason why we have to help the poor camp population with these extra rations. One cannot live on a watery soup with some vegetables floating in it, twice a day, a kind of brown water for breakfast called coffee and 250 grammes of bread (daily ration)! This is the usual menu in the camp. Making all allowances for the difficulty which the French commissary has in obtaining sufficient supplies, these are starvation rations.

In all the camps are cases of hunger edema and scurvy and T.B. cases are increasing rapidly. Thanks to the Quaker feeding the situation has ameliorated considerably but the difficulties would reappear immediately if we should stop the feeding, especially as winter is approaching.

Appendix

I wish I could give you an impression of what one hears in the camps about the Quaker food and how it is appreciated by the doctors and the internees. I visit Gurs myself once a month and am very satisfied with the efficient way in which our distribution is done there. As you may know we have a barrack of our own there in which the stock is kept and the supplies given out daily for the different îlots. They get now 65 to 75 grammes of dry food which make a thick soup of either chick-peas or beans or bean flour with noodles or rice or barley and milk. This is mixed with fresh vegetables provided by us. This soup reaches 1200 people daily, formerly from the districts of Palatine and Baden. The sick and old of Gurs have now been transferred to Noé and Récébédou where we have a similar feeding scheme from which all the Jewish internees profit. In Vernet, we have started with 400 daily extra meals and would like to increase the number. We do not feel that we should change this program or should discontinue in Gurs. Rivesaltes has a death rate of 48 daily, mostly children and babies, caused by undernourishment. We are glad to tell you that a similar feeding plan has been started for 4000 children in this camp. In all these camps, the feeding is supervised by the Quakers and regular weekly or bi-weekly visits made according to their location.

The problem of clothes and medical supplies is a great one. Only when one visits the camps regularly can one realize the immense need for help and the human misery engulfing the great number of foreigners in France.

Imagine many barracks full of people who are idle and confined within the limit of their îlot, though completely deprived of privacy. What the daily Quaker soup means to these people, not only because of their hunger, but for the spirit in which it is given!

We receive many letters of thanks for small services rendered which give back to these poor broken and persecuted people the faith in mankind and humanity.

I hope I have given you an idea of life in the camp and shown you the absolute necessity of continuing the feeding scheme, not only in Gurs but also in Noé, Récébédou, Vernet and Rivesaltes.

With my kind regards, yours sincerely,

C. Bleuland van Oordt

More letters from Papi, Mutti and Oma to Ernst and me at La Maison des Pupilles

April 30, 1941

My Dear Children!

I received your letter of April 22, the day before yesterday. Dear *Mutti* and I thank you very much for it. Most of all we were glad to hear that Ernstele and you are well. It also makes me happy that Ernstele plays in the yard with his car that was given to him here. Always write in detail about both of you so that we are informed - and let us know if the package and the money arrived. I am sending you a parcel again today: 1 green shirt, 1 pair of underpants, 2 pairs of socks and sweets from our dear *Mutti* and also an enclosure from Uncle Muni. Hopefully it will arrive soon. Enjoy the tasty content. Also, the relatives in Limoge wrote that they sent something to you. I am enclosing a pre-addressed, stamped envelope so that you can thank them for it. You write that you wait for mail. Hopefully my last letter was received by you in the meantime. *Oma* has a swollen face but she wants me to tell you that she will write to you as soon as she is well again - in the meantime, she sends her love. Otherwise everything here is as usual. The weather is good and I heard it is the same by you, so you will be able to get outdoors. Are you learning well and how do you spend your time? When do you go to bed and what more can you tell us? Write again in detail. *Opa* and Aunt Johanna also wrote and they are well and send regards and kisses. Best regards from Uncle Muni. My dear children, stay well, and write soon. Greetings and kisses from your loving Papi

Please send regards to Mr. and Mrs. Cohn. I forgot to mention that dear *Mutti* is still in the infirmary but she feels better.

Be Happy, Be Free, Dance!

My dear Boys:

We enjoyed your letter very much. Have fun at your playtime and go outdoors often. When you eat chocolate don't bite into it as your teeth might break. Hopefully you are well and happy. I feel better and send you only heartfelt greetings and kisses, my dear Richardle and Ernstele. Your loving *Mutti*

Best regards to Mrs. Cohn.

Undated - Illegible postmark

My Dear Richardle and My Dear Ernstele,

Many thanks for your lines. We are always pleased to hear that you enjoy it so much there. It is good to be with so many children. Do you have nice beds and do you sleep together? Do you, dear Richardle, have lessons or do you only play? Do you both already speak some French? Do you have friends yet? Do eat much so that you will grow tall. How is the weather? Are you often outdoors? Dear Richardle, when you have your writing day, please answer my questions. Ernstele, are you still the chief of your section? My dear children, hearty kisses from your loving *Mutti*

Best regards and kisses from your ever-loving *Papi*

Postcard
Sender: Max Weilheimer
Camp de Gurs, German Sect.
Ilot B, Barrack 11
Basses Pyrénées
5/41

Dear Children!

I hope that this finds you well. I was very happy to receive your drawing and your letter of 5/15/41. Both are very pleasing. Did you receive the overcoat and clothing in the meantime? They are all from Mr. Gimbel as are the paints. Uncle Muni sends regards, and he will write to you soon himself. What did you get to eat when you were invited to the countryside? Mr. and Mrs. Cohn have told us many good things about you. I sent you a little package and included shoelaces and polish. *Oma* is well and *Mutti* feels better.

Many hearty greetings and kisses, your loving
Papi

My Dear Children!

We were glad to receive your letter, dear Richardle. You and Ernstele wrote that a family invited you and you had a good time. Did you get something good to eat? What did you receive from the Quakers? Do you hike often? Is everything well with you? Did Ernstele gain weight and you, dear Richardle, did you grow? You drew so nicely; I kept the picture safely. Make us happy often and draw us pictures. Perhaps you can sketch your playroom or bedroom so that we can get a better idea where you live.

Greetings, your loving *Mutti*

May 16, 1941

My Dear Boys!

I received your letter yesterday, dear Richardle, and I thank you for it. I am happy that you are healthy, as that is always most important. It's great that Ernstele gained weight, and now you must gain also. Mrs. Cohn is here again, and she told me many nice things about you. *Mutti* and I were very happy about that. I still could not get a lock, it would be best if you can have someone buy one there. I am glad that you received the package and that its contents tasted good to you both. I think we can send you another parcel next week. We will write to you weekly but

Be Happy, Be Free, Dance!

I hear that you are now only allowed to write every fifteen days. Uncle Muni thanks you for your letter. He will write himself (—CENSORED—) still lies in the infirmary, but we hope for an improvement soon. You asked what we do all day long. As always, I have many chores before my daily visits to dear *Mutti*. My dear children, stay healthy and be good. Regards and kisses, your loving *Papi*

My Dear Children! Many hearty kisses, your loving *Mutti*. *Good shabbos.*

Postmarked 6/17/41

My Dear Children!

Hopefully this finds you in good health as is likewise the case with us. What is new with you? Please write again in detail and let Ernstele dictate something for us, as we always enjoy receiving news from you. Also, please answer our various questions which we asked in our last letter. What do you get to eat? Do you always get enough? Stay well, let us hear from you soon again. Hearty greetings and kisses from your loving *Papi*

My Dear Boys!

We just received your letter of June 11 and thank you very much. Ernstele dictated very nicely. Did you read a lot in both your books? Is the rabbit picture book nice? Write soon again. Your loving *Mutti*

Regards and kisses from *Oma* and Uncle Muni.

Appendix

Meine heissgeliebten Kinderchen! Freitag, den 26. Juni 1942.

Ich hoffe Euch bei bestem Wohle, Gleiches ist auch bei mir der Fall. Nachdem ich am Mittwoch noch einen schönen Tag mit Euch verleben durfte, es war aber leider viel zu kurz, seid Ihr gestern, Donnerstag, den 25.6.42. Nachm. 4 Uhr in See gegangen. Leider liess man mich nicht mehr zum Dampfer, ich hätte Euch zu gern gar nochmals gesehen und gesprochen. Und denkt Euch, ich fuhr am Nachmittag zur Mole. Car den Hafen und sah Euer Schiff liegen, die Frechheit, leider kam ich aber nur bis zum Gitter, etwa 200 Meter vom Dampfer entfernt. Um 4 Uhr sah ich wie die Landungsbrücke eingeholt und die Anker und Teile gezogen wurden und kurz darnach wurde Euer Schiff durch einen kleinen Schlepper hinausgezogen. Leute standen am Kai, um verabschiedeten sich und winkten und ich konnte, bedauerlicher Weise, nicht dabei sein. Bald war das Schiff entschwunden. Meine Stimmung war bei Euch. Also meine lieben, braven Kinderchen, nun wünsche ich Euch, nochmals alles Gute und vor allem Gesundheit. Reist mit Gott, möge er Euch beschützen und vor allem dem gesund erhalten. Möge er Euch einer frohen und glücklichen Zukunft entgegenführen und möge er Euch zu gegradas jüdischer Jungens heranwachsen lassen, die in dieser harten Welt ihren Mann stellen können. Ihr seid ja beide so lieb, brav und anständig erzogen, sodass Ihr euch überall beliebt machen könnt und gerne gesehen werdet. Von allen Leuten hier, die Euch, meine lieben Kinderchen, kennen, soll ich Euch grüssen und sie wünschen Euch alles Gute. Ich freue mich, wenn Ihr wieder bei unseren Lieben seid und dort wieder ein eigenes gutes Heim bekommt. Ich selbst hoffe baldigst zu Euch zu kommen, das alles ist im Sinne unserer guten lieben Mutti, die wir nie vergessen wollen und können, gerne wäre auch sie mit uns gefahren, Gott hat es anders gewollt. Ich sah auch wie bei Eurer Abfahrt ein Wasserflugzeug über Euer Dampfer kreuzte. Ich sende nun diese Zeilen Euch sofort durch Flugzeug zu damit Ihr bei Ankunft einen Gruss von mir habt. Ich bete täglich zu Gott für Euch und Eure Abfahrt, die sicherlich gut vorüber

Be Happy, Be Free, Dance!

EULOGY FOR LILLY WEILHEIMER - GURS, 7/20/41

A man's days are like grass, like a flower of the field he withers. Dear mourners, with aching heart, in recent days, husband and mother stood at the sickbed with the anxious question in their hearts: How much longer? For months a terrible affliction gnawed at the body of the all too early deceased. And we all admired the patience with which she bore her affliction. We meet many people during these difficult months of internment, but only a few impress us like this person who now left us. I will not forget the moment when I first met her. On a Friday evening in the winter in the infirmary of *îlot* F when I began to sing the *"Zaddik Kattomor"* in our familiar way, she began to sing the alto part with a beautiful voice; and when I went over to her at the end, her eyes glowed with gratitude. And since that Friday, with only one interruption, she always beautified the Friday evening service with her song. And how happy she was when her husband was allowed to take the place of the head of house and could sing the Kiddush (blessing over wine) the way she was accustomed from home. She came from a family of teachers. Her father, who was a teacher and cantor in Ludwigshafen for 30 years, educated her in the spirit of our Jewish teachings. And just as, for generations, the family dedicated itself to our profession, she also chose children's education as her profession. And those who were privileged to know her sunny disposition know that she was eminently qualified for this profession. In the family in which she worked professionally, she was accepted like a child of the family. And when she managed a Kindergarten in her hometown, she was "Aunt Lilly," who was admired and loved by all. And with how much pride and how much motherly love she showed me the beautiful pictures of her own two children who now, unfortunately, much too early, have to do without the mother's love.

So her mother and her husband are left to continue the legacy of the deceased, care for the children and give them a good Jewish education. And it was characteristic of her husband's and her mother's good Jewish convictions that, in conversation with me, they felt that their first and most important task was to get the children a new home as soon as possible with their Aunts in America. This is the Jewish duty, to resignedly accept God's decree and not to let the pain disconcert you, but, in the spirit of the deceased, to continue the task that she considered the most important of her life.

Therein may be a consolation for her stricken mother and her sorely tried husband. They stood around the sickbed in tireless care and love and did all they could to lighten her difficult lot! Now that she left us, we must replace the love of a mother's heart for the children, who were so attached to her.

This homegoing also means a big loss for her acquaintances and comrades. Whoever knew the dear departed had to love her. And she was treated with special love and devotion by the infirmary personnel who did everything possible, in these primitive conditions, to help the sick one. For all of them, the death of the dear departed is a painful loss.

In the forthcoming [Torah] portion we read *sidrah Mattot Maasey* (at the end of the book of Numbers). It recounts all the ordeals that our people had to endure on their trip through the desert. We, too, had to start on a painful road. And, just as our mother Rachel died on the way without having reached her destination, so also our dear departed left us before she was allowed to reach her destination, a new home for her dear ones and herself! So we salute you now for the last time. Go in peace.

From dust you came, and to dust you will return.
Amen